MISTER
A Dublin Childhood

Contents

Michael O'Beirne

One day the master said we were to write a comp on
'Ireland, my own country'. I was glad of that, as my
favourite subject was English.

Far Room
and
Little Room

Clearing out a few odds and ends the other day I came on this old-fashioned fancy button. I picked it up casually, then smoothing off dust with my thumb, I began to remember. As it lay in my hand the little amber dome twinkled with gold specks within its gloss — the same fiery life I'd marvelled at as a small boy. It awakened memories that went back sixty years, to 1916 and still further back, and in a mood of reverie I relived childhood days.

'Always dry between your toes first,' mother said, 'then you'll never catch a cold.' She lifted me soap-slippy from the galvanised iron bath and plonked me on a towel in front of the red fire. Every Saturday me and Joe, my young brother, had a bath in the far room, before *he* would arrive home from work.

First mother fiercely scrubbed my head and body with the towel, then I'd be sitting with both knees cocked up, doing my toes. I was four. A velvet glow came from the coal fire where a saucepan bubbled, for at weekends we had a special dinner, cabbage and pig's cheek.

We lived in Dublin, in Ireland, at the top of a highly respectable house in Clare Street near Merrion Square. Myself and Joe were often over at the window gazing the whole length of the street, the sunny side, from Gilbey's corner to the Mont Clare hotel. On that corner, the one near the Square, there stood a small red pillar with a window you could smash. It said: 'In case of Fire break glass; fine five pounds.'

It was winter, with Christmas coming soon. In summer the roofs of the houses opposite had purple slates and a blue sky, but now the roofs were white with frost and nearer, bright against the louring, purple clouds. Spiky Jack Frost furrowed the window pane.

My forehead felt cold against the glass as I peeped from tiptoe down at the small hall-doors and area railings rising into view, and even, reflected

1

in D. H. Charles the solicitor's window, our own shadowy hall-door and a bit of our shop — it really belonged to Miss Carney Ladies' Outfitter, who was all business in a long black skirt and blouse. The landlord was Major Lindsay, but you could go down to Miss Carney with the rent and the book, and she would mark it off, paid.

You could see the pavement far below, and the dumpy men and women who were going by. Their arms hung down, their hands and feet kept going in and out. It was great, and a Dalkey tram would clatter past with its hissing trolly and red wooden seats on top. Sometimes the *boom-a-boom* of a big drum brought us rushing to see the soldiers marching on their way, all the legs in step together with their pulsing band. *One-two, left-right*, it was 1914 and the army was recruiting for the war.

We could do more than look out at the world. On the far chimney-pots there would be sea-gulls which came screaming, enormous white staring things, to gobble bread off the window-sill and wing away with their piercing wails. We could make the same screech by rubbing the window with a cork —*Yiii!-yih-yih-yih*—*Yiii!-yih-yih-yih*—

Our part of the house, the top, had three rooms and a long landing. The door of the Far Room had no knob, only a grimy round hole. Beside this room was the bedroom, but this had nothing in it only two beds, the window and the wash-stand. You could walk along the landing where *he* had his carpenter's bench and his toolbox, under the skylight, all with a musk woody smell. We were closed in from the rest of the house by a timber partition which had a peep-hole my mother used for peeping through, down into the dark well of the stairs with its criss-cross of banister rails and flights of bare steps.

If mother heard anybody coming up she'd peep at them before they knocked at the cross door; she would know then whether to answer the knock or keep quiet. She'd make a sign to us, finger to lips. Beside the cross door was the Little Room, where my granny and aunt Maggie lived. The door of this room had a proper, shiny brass knob. When the door was locked I could rattle the knob, and being good I was always allowed in. It was a tidy room with a fender in front of the fire, and we had peace and quiet.

Already, in the far room, there were Merry Christmas mottoes hung up. We had our dinner early on Saturdays before *he* arrived at half-past one, his usual time. *He* was my father. The name Father seems odd, because we never used it. My mother spoke of him as 'he' or 'him', or 'that fellow', and she addressed him as 'Mister'. Of course he called her 'Missus' and spoke of 'the missus', but somehow that sounded all right.

2

Myself and my Nana O'Reilly.

There was a crash and mother said, 'That's him.' Although the cross door was locked he had a way of shoving it open. We heard his heavy step along the landing.

The moment he came into the room my mother started talking. It was disturbing the way she talked, all in a rush, not waiting for an answer: 'Ah there you are Mister your dinner is ready. Did you have a hard day you must be tired out. I suppose you'll be in a hurry to get away to the first house here's your dinner — you like the bit of pig's cheek it's tasty a lovely bit I got in Moore Street.'

'Tunder has it in for me all right,' my father said. He said 'Tunder', but it was really Thunder, a funny name. That was his boss in the Maintenance Department of the Dublin Corporation. 'He has me running from billy to jack,' my father said grumpily.

'Are you telling me that, now,' mother said. 'You must be starving with the hunger Mister have a bit to eat.'

My father sat down at the table with his coat off, and his face looked grim. He rolled his shirt-sleeves back from hairy arms and started eating, sitting near the fire and talking, at first mildly.

'There's nothing like the bit of pig's cheek,' he said, chewing. Swallowing the mouthful, he continued, angrily:

'They treat me like a dog. First I'm told go to the Pigeon House, then Tunder sends me back. I wouldn't have minded so much,' my father said, 'only Kettle comes down the stairs, and the lady typist after him. "What's this man doing here?" he says to Tunder — this is *me*! "What's this man doing here?" And the lady typist listening!'

'Musha what harm is that,' my mother said, frowning. 'Have another bit and you'll feel better sure tomorrow's another day. I'll have your tea in a minute, the kettle's boiling. You'll be in a hurry to get out, Mister, maybe the Tivoli or something to kill a few hours.'

It was queer the way mother chattered but he didn't seem to notice. But the way she frowned, talking, you could see she was annoyed about the lady typist. Mother often told us — me and Joe — that before she got married she was considered a great beauty. What was a lady typist? When mother worked in the sweet-shop the men all called her Gabrielle Raye, after the stage actress. What a beautiful name! There were even photo-postcards of Miss Raye in a white floppy hat, with a neck like a swan and big eyes and luxuriant tresses.

'I might as well mosey off out,' my father said. 'It'll break the monotony.'

'Do, do Mister,' mother said quickly. 'Sure you might as well have some enjoyment the house is a killer.' She smiled encouragement at him to go.

We heard him walking down the lobby and slamming the cross door. After that Joe spoke up: 'Will Mister be coming back?'

Mother said, suddenly gay: 'He'll be back soon enough, like a bad penny.' She chanted: 'Christmas is coming and the geese are getting fat... Come on, kids, sit at the fire and I'll tell yous about Christmas.'

You'd forget about everything listening to Christmas, what it would be like. Mother would go out on Christmas Eve and get all kinds of guldies and toys and cake and a goose and everything in Moore Street. One of the weeks before that she brought us with her. All the oul ones were shouting 'Are you buying, ma'am — only tuppence a pound here the spanished onions.'

'What are you asking for the apples?' mother would say — and offer half the price. Maggie said she was a great one for bargaining, as bad as the oul ones themselves. She said they hated mother.

We turned into Cole's Lane, and at one of the stalls there mother bought me a new calico suit. I was to wear it on Sunday and have my photo taken, not tomorrow or Saturday, but on Sunday after Mass.

In the Far Room there were chairs, the table, a sofa, and a bed for Joe and me. It was all right to waken up on weekday mornings. I could see the fire lighting, a leg of the table, the over-mantel of red-and-yellow oilcloth and a motto *Home Sweet Home*. He would be there, so I'd pretend to be asleep till he had gone to work. He was a carpenter and had to go out early.

Sunday was different from other days. That morning, across the roofs would roll the mournful clang, clang of the chapel bell. It was the morning my father would be home, standing with his back to our bed and staring in the mirror, shaving. He kept wiping the razor on a bit of *Evening Herald*. He would have nothing on but trousers and his braces hanging down.

My father was a boxer in spare time, the champion fly-weight. He had a photograph of himself in his boxing-knicks and shoes and boxing-gloves, taken by Tisdale. He looked well with his left glove and left foot forward and the chin protected by a hunched-up shoulder.

Being a boxer, my father would think nothing of stripping to the waist to shave. His eyes seemed to stare at me out of the mirror. Behind the soapy Santa Claus beard he grinned and grimaced to shave himself better, and his mouth made a black sideways *O* as he plucked up his nose from the open razor, shaving his lip.

My mother said there was a gentleman in the sweet-shop making up to her, but my father chased this fellow with an open razor along Harcourt

Street, and he only escaped by jumping on a tram at the last moment.

While the shaving was taking place there'd be the smell and buzz of rashers frying in the pan. He would put on his freshly-laundered shirt from the White Swan Laundry and sit down to his tea, rashers, and fried bread. With his back to the window his dark face looked darker, maybe a thread of grease gleaming on his chin.

Some of the happiest hours of my childhood were those I shared with my aunt Maggie and Nana, my granny. Of course I was there only on sufferance — after all I was one of 'that crew', as Nana called those in the Far Room. I was tolerated, and was careful not to do or say anything that would spoil my welcome.

Nana was a gentle, frail old lady whose black silk blouse had often the gold dust of snuff to be flicked off. She wore glasses, and one of her eyes veered sideways giving her a shocked expression. Her father Captain Archbold, skipper of a cargo vessel, had been suffocated in his cabin by a charcoal fire.

In the Little Room all was quietness and ordinary talk, though at times aunt Maggie could be raging. Now and again, coming home from her work at the bookfolding, aunt Maggie would say 'I'm only raging,' and proceed to recount the latest happening. The forewoman, Miss Helena Moloney, was a proper targer, Maggie said. By times she had a tongue like a fish-woman, and then again at her most ladylike she could give you a deliberate cut.

I often wondered what it was that made big people so cross and sad. My aunt and granny seemed milder than most. If it came to tea-time I would be given a place at the table with its white cloth and bone-china cups and saucers. It was lovely listening to the rhythmic, melancholy murmur of aunt Maggie and my granny talking.

A few times I even had dinner in the Little Room. It was nice and tasty anyhow — perhaps a coddle of rashers and sausage boiled up. I remember Maggie remarking, with a laugh: 'I like onions, but alas, they don't like me.'

Granny nodded and said: 'Onions often repeat.' (This was called 'breakin' a pudden'.)

From a turn in the talk it appeared that I hadn't always lived in Clare Street. At first they had a flat in Baggot Street, and amazingly it was in Baggot Street I was born.

'Everything was nice there, I'll say that for her.' Maggie said. 'Ah well, if you want to know me come and live with me. The day he polished the boots — a Sunday morning — and put one of his hooverils up on the

6

beautiful antimacassar chair!'

Nana shook her head. 'That finished him with her.'

'From the first I seen of him I knew he was no class,' Maggie said. 'But would she listen? You might as well talk to the wall. How right I was! Sure even his brother Paddy as good as told her—'

'Whisht — spiro!'

Granny only murmured 'spiro', meaning to shut up he's listening. She was looking at me. I pretended not to notice — just unfolded my *Tiger Tim's Weekly* and asked Maggie would she read it out for me. This was what was known as providing a welcome diversion, besides not letting on that I had noticed 'spiro'.

'Musha,' granny said, 'ain't the evenings drawing in.'

It was nearly too dark to read, my aunt would have to light the lamp. At first she would light it only dimly till the globe got warm, then she would raise the wick. While Maggie turned the little knob I looked expectantly at Nana. Nearly always she'd be sure to bless herself and mildly remark: 'God send us the light of heaven.'

How cosy it was there, nearly as bright as day with the lamp lighting and the blind drawn down. We would sit around the fire, me in my small wicker armchair, they in their big ones, and Maggie would be reading out the *Evening Mail*, or *Adam Bede*, or *A Tale of Two Cities*. On this occasion, after lots of coaxing, she was reading out my *Tiger Tim's*.

Merrion Square from Clare Street. The first house on the left was Oscar Wilde's birthplace.
The Shelbourne Hotel on St Stephen's Green East, around 1916.

Sunday Visitors

On rare occasions in those early days we had a Sunday visitor. We might come home from Mass — me and Joe and him, that is — and find that uncle Paddy had arrived. This was a welcome event in the stodgy uneventfulness of Sunday morning. We children at first kept a respectful distance, examining the stranger with attentive awe. He would be in the Far Room, sitting down, when I came in.

Uncle Paddy, my father's brother, was always aunt Maggie's favourite. Say what you like, he was a perfect gentleman, he had a nice clean trade in the bookbinding, and like that again he was a total abstainer.

I rose into the air between his hands once, and was put sitting on his knee. You could see that my uncle Paddy was a nice man. He even smelled nice. When he took out his rubber pouch to fill his pipe the smell was even better. He sucked his cheeks in, lighting the pipe fiery-red with a match, and puffed out smoke. He had a skinny nose, black eyebrows, a moustache like black wires.

Uncle Paddy wore a beautiful blue suit, and across his waistcoat in two loops a silver chain. When he took his watch out to see the time a silver lid flipped open. He let me listen to the tick.

'Go on, listen to the tick. Hold it to your ear and listen.'

It was a shiny watch, with a bulging glass that you could put your finger on and press, and still the little beetle-mark moved on, round and round. That was uncle Paddy's silver watch, back in his waistcoat pocket.

'Heigh hoe!' he said. 'Time and tide wait for no man.' He stood up and looked at me with sharp, staring brown eyes. 'I'll slip in next door and say hello to Maggie.' When Paddy stood up and put on his bowler hat it made him look stern.

We had another visitor one Sunday evening, after dinner. This was my father's mother Roseanna, a sort of grandmother of mine who lived in

9

York Street. She had been over in the church to say a prayer for us and all poor sinners. She was fat, with a red face and pale hairs growing out of her chin.

'Well thanks be to God!' Roseanna said, flopping down on a chair. 'Yous were better off in Baggot Street them stairs has me killed.' She used to wear a black balloon of a hat, and in no time she'd have one arm on the table and the drop of stout beside her.

Roseanna had a soft spot for Joe, who was a jolly little chap with golden curls. She would put her arms out and coax him up on her lap with a wheezy, 'Ah, Dod love him!' Joe laughed up in her face as she jogged him on her knee, in time to her jiggy song of:

Ha, ha, ha — he, he, he!
Little brown jug don't I love thee!

My mother found a cup for Roseanna to pour her stout in, and was looking for another for herself. 'I only brung the two bottles,' my strange granny said. 'He never looks at it himself, he hates the sight of it.'

My father was sitting at the fire too, reading the racing page and taking no notice. Mother kept moving around, eagerly asking Roseanna how she was, and how Paddy was, and did she ever hear from John — that was the other married son; but at last my new granny exclaimed in a hoarse, plaintive tone: 'Woman dear, can't you sit down! I'll tell you what's wrong with you, missus, like it or lump it — it's your nerves.'

'That's one thing about Mick there,' Roseanna said, pointing out my father, 'he must have nerves of iron. He can draw a straight line freehand, you'd swear he used a ruler. Of course he never done the mensuration at school but it seems to come natural.'

'Will you shut up?' my father said.

Roseanna went on: 'Ever tell you the time Brother Coyne got on to him for using a ruler when he shouldn't of? "You used a ruler!" says Brother Coyne. "I did not!" says your man. Neither a one would give in. Well, whenever your man says "I did not!" the Brother slapped him. They kep at it: "You did!" — slap! "I did not!" "You did!" — slap! "I did not!" "You did!" — slap! His poor hands was riz from the weltin'.'

'Aw, will you give over,' my father said gruffly.

'They'd be at it yet,' said Roseanna. 'I suppose the bell must of went.'

Mother wouldn't sit down, but kept giving Roseanna a nice polite smile. 'Haven't you all the luck,' mother said, 'with two sons like Paddy and John.'

10

'Huh! I'm sure they're fetttin' about me — sure Paddy is always out fishin' and diggin' up lug-worms, and John is married this five year.'

Roseanna began to talk and boast about the fine home uncle John had, across on the north side of the city. My father sat hunched over the fire, and once or twice when staring at his mother his redflecked brown eyes quivered.

'A whole house he has of his own,' Roseanna said, 'across in Church Street. Green and cream vases on the mantel-piece, and in the window a cut-glass bowl between two spotless curtains.'

'See that now!' mother said. 'We have lace curtains too.'

'Ah, but you should see his house. You should visit his home, ma'am, see his missus and beautiful children, it would do your heart good!'

'We have full and plenty, all anybody wants,' my father said. 'I have a steady job.'

'So you should have, like your father Bernard before you — as I told them in the Corporation,' Roseanna said, 'when I brung you there at fourteen and got you a trade.'

'I was fully entitled. I was teached by the Brothers and I got my due I was fully entitled to.'

'Go 'long you, wud your pitch-an'-toss schools and your nose near broke — you had the makings of a gutter fighter and a gambler. Missus, I seen the ruin risin' up before him and I got him a trade, thanks be to God, 'twas an answer to prayer.'

She must have got uncle Paddy his trade too. Paddy lived with his mother in York Street and that was strange, him being a perfect gentleman. Mother used to say about my father, what could you expect from York Street and its tenemented houses.

But this granny kept on about the wonderful home uncle John had, until my father began to growl and curse under his breath.

'Aw, wait'en I tell yous the best part of all — didn't John get a *manservant* — to wait on him! Waits on him hand and fut.'

At this news my father began to get really annoyed. Roseanna said: 'It's the Gospel truth I'm tellin' yous. A poor brokendown homeless old man that John, out of charity, took pity on. He has him in a white apron serving the dinner, calls him "My man" —'

'Shut up and get out! Get out, or by God I'll pitch you down them stairs!'

The noise was frightening the way my father shouted, banging the table till things fell from it and crashed and smashed, and the walls and floorboards quivered. My father had jumped up, mad with rage and

11

roaring curses at his mother.

'God blast you for a dirty busybody! Never satisfied till you cause trouble! You're a bloody mischief-maker, always was — get to hell out of it, wud your cut-glass and your man-servant! Coming here to raise a row, you oul cack, you. Blasted oul cow!'

'Name of the Father, Son and Holy Ghost!' Roseanna quavered, grabbing a watery glass jampot from the mantel. It was paraffin she took for Holy Water, sprinkling it over us, sprinkling the fireplace and the fire. Yellow flames flared up the chimney, burning soot blackened the hearth, and an ominous throb, throb in the chimney-flue grew louder as the flames leaped upward.

Someone must have seen the black smoke billowing, and read 'In case of Fire break glass.' Before we knew what was happening there crashed out a frenzy of ding-a-dong bells, and in burst the Fire Brigade in bright brass helmets, hauling a great hose the height of the house. The smoky room seemed full of big brass-hatted men. They all stood gazing at the hose and waiting, but only a dribble of water trickled out. The hose-bearer said in a flat, resentful tone: 'This is totally inadequate.' They began to roll up the flat hose, the fire having gone out by itself. 'It'll cost you five pounds,' one of the firemen said, 'if you bring us out again on a fool's errand.'

We watched in silence the twinkling helmets bobbing away down through the dark maze of banister-rails.

Ain't We Very Stupid!

My comic had follow-up pictures about Tiger Tim, a furry young tiger with black-and-red stripes on his body, legs and tail. He had a fat-faced cheeky grin and I admired him as a person as real, to me, as the breadman, Mr Boland.

Much as I admired Tiger Tim I had never supposed that he could actually come into my life. I had no desire to be like Tiger Tim, yet amazingly it happened! It was when Sunday arrived, the day for my photograph. Maggie was to take me to Mass, then all the way to Harcourt Street to Mr Tisdale's.

Mother said Maggie was a fusspot. She fumed and muttered, making me turn that way and this way, combing and brushing my hair, then red-faced with bending she tugged and smoothed my calico dress from collar to skirt. My boots had been polished. I was made to sit up on the bed to have my boots and socks put on.

'Sweet Lord! Are you trying to catch flies or what?' she panted, meaning keep your mouth shut. This was annoying to say the least, but it was nothing compared to the socks my aunt had bought, which I saw being pulled onto my feet and ankles. I choked with dismay and horror. The socks would turn me into Tiger Tim — because my legs, with the socks pulled up, would have black-and-red stripes!

My boots came up high enough to hide the tiger-stripes, but they were still there. My throat, face and eyes filled up with tears, and worst of all was knowing that it would be useless trying to explain. All the way to Mass I wept, often shaken roughly by my furious and mystified aunt, and all through Mass, and red-eyed, sobbing, all the way to Tisdale.

We entered the photographer's house, strangely quiet with its polished and carpeted stairs and thick folds of hangings at the top. When Maggie said 'Blow!' and held her hankie to my nose, I had forgotten Tiger Tim.

13

I was merely a small, dumbfounded child being led across the expanse of a carpeted room, and stood in front of wallpaper depicting urns of flowers backed by a garden.

'Hold that,' a man said, and gave me a basket of flowers. He stared at me and fixed me and the basket in position. A queer black-headed thing on spiky legs was there too, watching me with its glistening one eye.

'That's fine,' the photographer said when he had fixed me. 'Don't move, just listen to the birdie.'

He went in under a black cloth. I kept watching the shape of Mr Tisdale's head and listening for the bird to chirp, or chirrup. In vain. It was all over then — Mr Tisdale came out and smiled and said, again, 'That's fine.'

I could see nothing fine about it. No birdie, no photograph, and the man had even taken back my basket! It was a dark disappointment. As I was hurried home the grimness of real life allowed no time for thoughts of Tiger Tim. And everywhere there was the shut-shop dismalness of Sunday.

By degrees, from day to day I got to know the larger, outside world. When granny had heard me through morning prayers she'd send me down to McCarthy's for half an ounce of snuff, measured out in a tiny hammer-scoop. There were shops along our side of Clare Street, with part of the pavement sloping up to them. First a picture shop; then McKeever's Chemists; then Mr Marks the umbrella shop. McCarthy's papers and sweet-shop was next, then a sort of antique shop, and Greene's, the post-office and book-shop. After that, nothing but Moffey's Corner, where each evening Moffey in a cap and raincoat, with sleeves nearly hiding his pale hands, would stand calling 'Herrildy-Mail!'

On Monday mornings mother often brought me with her on her trip to the pawn-office with a 'bundle'. Inside the paper covering would be his Sunday suit wrapped in a sheet for safety.

Moffey would be at his corner calling out the morning paper: 'Inna-pennant — Innapennant!' One time mother shushed me as we passed and I called out! 'There's Moffey!' He only smiled and winked: 'Them kids 'ud hang you.'

We'd go round Moffey's Corner, along Merrion Square, past the sedate Duke's Lawn and into Baggot Street. On the left side of Baggot Street we pretended to walk past the pawn-office as though we didn't even see the three brass balls. Mother always cut in by the side entrance in Rock Lane. Her pawn-office name was 'McCabe'.

This bare musty place, mother said, was 'Uncle's'. This must be where uncle Paddy worked, I thought, watching, but saw only a worn wooden

Myself aged about six, 1916.

counter and a man in shirt sleeves. He took the parcel, opened it, pinned it up again and said, 'Five bob.'

'Ah, Paddy,' mother said coaxingly, 'make it the ten.'

'Five bob,' he said again. 'Name?'

'McCabe,' mother said, giving me a quick wink, as much to say, 'It isn't my real name, but it's good enough for that fellow!'

I stared amazed at this peculiar uncle Paddy, who not even once had looked at mother. 'McCabe!' he shouted to someone upstairs. He wrote on a slip of paper called the pawn ticket, scooped it through sand and gave the bristly scrawl to mother with five shillings. Our bundle was flung into a wooden lift, a rope was pulled and up it trundled, Paddy shouting after it, 'Gent's blue in white!' It was wonderful to see his good suit going up like that, away up, then gone.

After all there was a photograph. At dinner-time, having a standing-up cup of tea Maggie said she could just manage Tisdale's in the lunch-hour, and right enough she arrived home that evening with a little tissue paper parcel. It was a brown mounted print of me holding a basket of flowers. Chubby-cheeked and open-mouthed I was watching for the dickie bird with sad attentive eyes. Ringlets hid both my ears, and in the calico smock I looked just like a girl.

Despite the flower-basket photo I was really a boy — as the following Sunday revealed. Because the next thing Maggie did was to bring me visiting to show off my new dress and polished boots. It seemed I had another aunt who lived on the North Strand, my aunt Crissy McCabe. We went in a tram to visit her.

The McCabes lived in a terrace of small houses, but their parlour, inside, looked enormous. In this room of mahogany furniture all went very well, at first. We got tea and cake and they were talking, but the wonderful part of it was the two girls who were there, sitting with us in the parlour.

These girls were my cousins, Crissy and Maisie McCabe, and they were washed. Crissy was about my own age and Maisie a bit older, but Crissy had fluffy fair hair and a sweet smile. I fell in love with her at once.

'Crissy'. It was by far the best name any girl could have. I felt afraid to look at her. She sat on the nearest high plush chair and the coloured soft frock showed the soft curvy shape of her legs going up under her skirt. I decided I would like to marry Crissy.

'Ain't we very stupid!'

With her two eyes fixed on me, the aunt Crissy said this to Maggie. I stared back at her. No doubt she had said something to me that I never heard, or perhaps asked me a question. Well I had heard the sly thing she

16

said about ain't we stupid — out loud, as if I wouldn't know! I was only raging but there was nothing I could say, so I just glared at her. Anyway, she would see that I *did* know, now!

I took a terrible turn against that aunt. Even though her name was Crissy, in her case it was dark and different. I hated that old black Crissy as much as I loved the young, fair-haired Crissy, the memory of whose glistening curls and sunny smile would linger with me. The two Crissys were mixed up in my mind in a confusing way, and they seemed to be saying, with two pairs of eyes fixed on me: 'Ain't you very stupid!'

My brother Joe, the second eldest of the family.

Terror

'Christmas is coming and the geese are getting fat,
Who'll put a penny in the poor man's hat?'

We heard a lot about it, but the time leading on to Christmas went slowly,
more like a year than a month. One morning I was told to take Joe with
me and play in the Duke's Lawn. When we got back a strange woman in a
cloak was coming down the stairs. She smiled at me and said: 'You have
a new little sister.'

Intense joy hurried me on. Then, not to seem too eager, I walked slowly
along the lobby to the far room. Timidly I pushed the door, saw it
receding little by little and the view of the room widening. The leather-
covered sofa, worn leather-seated chairs, the table, the end of my bed and
the mirror beyond it shining. But nobody there!

She must be hiding from me. There was only one possible place, a
curtained alcove by the window. Almost dancing with delight I crossed the
room. I pictured her, a little girl with golden curls dressed in a short white
frock, and as I pulled aside the curtain she would chuckle gleefully.

A pang of disappointment — the curtain fell back in still folds. But they
were calling. I went running to the bedroom. On the bed lay my mother,
turning towards me her smiling white face. Open-mouthed I stood gazing
at the tiny, squeezed-up face beside her, red against a pale, smooth breast.
The little scowling face was sucking and the doll-sized fingers clutching.
Under the bed was the bath we were washed in on Saturday mornings,
nearly full of crimsoned water. With a feeling of disgust I turned and left
the room.

At long last Christmas came. There was a tall red candle on the mantel-
piece. There were glossy mottoes on the walls. *A Happy Xmas, Christmas
Greetings to All*, and red-berried holly overhung the pictures. A huge iron

19

pot, always borrowed from Mrs Hayes in the opposite house at Christmas, bubbled on our fire which glowed from hob to hob. Even the new baby, in bed, had watched mother making the pudding, and we all got glimpses of the swelling cloth with water boiling round it.

There were pieces of wood on the hearth, and my father showed Joe and me how to build them up criss-cross, the way a crow builds her nest. It went up, up, up, and he said: 'There's your crow's nest.'

After that he was sitting away from the fire in his shirt sleeves; it would roast you. On the table parcels were piled high, in the midst of them a white goose with its fat legs sticking up. We children played on the floor while mother went back and forward overhead, laughing and talking. My father, in the best of humour, held a newspaper spread out from one hand, and the blue smoke of his cigarette curled upward through its shadow.

Soon after the candle was lit we had to be in bed. I lay there thinking of my sock pinned to the brass rail, and wondering about Santa Claus. Mother said he would surely come, and would come down the chimney. Guiltily I wondered were they waiting till we were fast asleep to come and fill our socks. I pretended to be asleep and must have drifted off, for suddenly it was the chilly dark of morning. I put a hand up to the crinkly, mysterious bulge above my head with marvelling excitement.

On Christmas Day he brought Joe and me to visit his mother Roseanna, in York Street. We passed by the open hall-doors of tall old houses, and came to a dark, musty hall. 'You could drive a coach-and-four through this,' my father said. It was a gloomy, vast, bare house.

Inside Roseanna's large room there was a bird under glass, two great windows, a sewing-machine, a bed at either end and lots of furniture. As usual the granny said, embracing us: 'Dod love yous!' There were kittens playing on a bed, furry kittens with bright watchful eyes. We played with them and I was sorry when we had to leave.

At home that Christmas night there was a visitor, in fact two visitors. Mr Breen, my father's friend, who made leather leggings, had brought along a gentleman named Captain MacBride. They all had a sort of sing-song. First Captain MacBride, with Joe up on his knee, gave us the *Sean Van Vocht:*

Oh the French are on the say,
Says the Sean Van Vocht—
They'll be here without delay,
And the orange will decay—
Oh the French are on the say,
Says the Sean Van Vocht.

My father and Mr Breen joined in the chorus, it was better than a band, then Mr Breen asked my father if he knew a thing called 'Thora'.

'I do. Yes, that's a lovely thing,' my father said, and when the other two clapped he sang 'Thora'. What I remember best of that evening is my father singing 'Asleep in the Deep', it was powerful. I never knew my father had a rumbley, saddened voice to sing like that.

After a while there was nothing but talk, so I went into Nana's room. They were in great good-humour there as well, and Maggie had a box of chocs and gave me one. I had supper with Nana and my aunt. Sitting in their cosy room, it was nice to know that in the Far Room they were warm and cosy too.

A few days later he was back at work again. Mother had a hacking cough on account of the bitter-cold weather, so leaving Joe and Meg — our new sister — with granny, she brought me out with her to the dispensary. We turned right from Lincoln Place into Denzille Street, a real low-class locality of tenemented houses with the washing all hung out from windows.

Quickly we trotted along to the dispensary in Grand Canal Street. A lot of sick people were sitting on wooden benches outside the doctor's room. He kept banging a bell. Each patient hurried in, hurried out, then our turn came. Mother had a little song for it:

'Come in, come on,
Put out your tongue,
What's your name and
Have you the bottle?

We got the brown cough mixture and mother's next stop was Cashel the coalman in Cumberland Street. She ordered coal in this rat-hole of a shop, where the gloom-enclosed, shadowy family showed white eyes and teeth grinning through coal-dust.

Crossing to Lincoln Place I thought mother was making for McGrane's the chandlers, but instead, hesitating a little, she stepped into Sweeny's chemist. She whispered something to the small, dusty-haired man and he said, sharply, 'Let me see it.'

My mother glanced down at me, then going nearer the counter she opened the top of her coat, and the jacket under that, and her blouse. The little chemist kept watching keenly through his specs.

Mother said, very low: 'It's like a boil. It has me nearly out of my mind, but I dread getting it lanced.'

'I've no faith in them surgeons,' Mr Sweeny said gruffly. 'Any arse or ache, it's all the same to them — the knife. I tell you what I'll do.' He

21

turned away, then back. 'Here's a good long bit of bandage. Put a bread-and-water poultice on that breast morning and evening, hot as you can bear. You'll get relief all right, pull it out like a string when it's coming.'

My mother said 'God bless you for that!' She said the same to Mr Boland the breadman every Thursday when he lent her five shillings. The weekly loan was handy to see us through Thursday and Friday, repaid on Saturday.

It was nice going out with mother in the mornings, but even better were the evenings at home in Nana's room. You'd notice a little extra bright-ness every evening now, the cock's step. We had a high-barred fire with a betty around it, and its flames winked in the polished fender.

It always took me unawares when the chapel bell tolled out at six, to see Maggie standing up facing the altar. From behind would come the creak of granny's cane chair and we would all be standing.

'An angel of the Lord declared unto Mary,' Maggie would say; and granny answered: 'And she conceived of the Holy Ghost.' Then Maggie, the Hail Mary prayer, and us two the Holy Mary.

'Behold the handmaid of the Lord,' Maggie declaimed, 'Be it done unto me according to thy will.' Hail Mary, Holy Mary... Then Maggie gave a little bob in token of bending a knee, and we with her, at 'And the Word was made flesh, and dwelt amongst us.' That was a solemn and holy part but it was all over in a minute and we could sit down.

This was called the Angelus. I suppose after the Angel who appeared.

It would be coming up to tea-time now, too dark for reading, yet not dark enough to light the lamp. Between-lights it was called, when for a few minutes we could share the stillness of the evening, and the Sacred Heart lamp on the altar seemed to deepen the dusk with its ruby glow.

Soon enough you'd need to have the lamp lighting, and I used to listen for my father's footsteps going past the door. About five past six you'd hear the cross door slamming mildly and his footfalls going down the lobby to the Far Room. If my aunt happened to be reading the evening paper she would read on, with only the slightest pause.

It really was marvellous the way my aunt read out. We had the lamp behind us. Nana's eyes would close behind her steel-rimmed spectacles, a hand listless on her *Evening Herald*, maybe, and both of us listening. This would be after tea, and one of the books Maggie read was *Bleak House*. She would often stop to praise some interesting part, or maybe interrupt herself with a little exclamation, like 'The villainy of that!'. Nana would say, shaking her head sadly and staring at the fire, 'Ah, Dickens knew the world.' You could see two small red fires reflected in her glasses.

'Ah, them lawyers! No wonder 'tis said they only get to heaven by degrees.' Munching a chocolate, feet on the fender, Maggie would rub black-stockinged legs to cool them. 'Ah, well,' she would sigh, lifting up the book. Her voice took on the mournful, even chant with which she read aloud.

These evenings my father went out after his dinner. He went with a heavy, deliberate step, briefly slamming the door. Then one, two, three, four — he was gone. Occasionally in the evenings there would be a row. We would hear him shouting in the Far Room, and my mother's voice raised shrilly.

'H'm!' Maggie would say. 'We're off again.' She was nervous though she spoke disgustedly. Then he would go tramping past, slamming the door so that the lamp flickered.

'It's time you were in your bed.' Nana said to me. 'Be off with you now, and God bless.'

Evening after evening it seemed quite natural to slip into Nana's room and sit there like a good little boy. With my knees jutting up from the tub-shaped wicker armchair I stared at the fire while Maggie read to Nana. I felt sad. It was easy to see that I was growing up, growing old. Hairs on my legs gleamed gold in the firelight and my knees looked enormous, getting too big for my velveteen pants. The thought of becoming a man filled me with dread.

Not even the adventures of Tiger Tim were all that interesting, but I listened while Maggie read out one of them. It was really quite good, but as Maggie was reading the door burst open and my mother rushed in, followed by my father. He was glaring and shouting. He hit my mother and her face went white.

'Get out! Get out to hell!' my father shouted.

Maggie tried to hold his arm. My mother's face was the colour of bread. She stood rigidly before him, screaming: 'I'll brain him!' My father cursed her. I felt my legs trembling. In the uproar of noise and curses my aunt's voice could now and then be heard, all the words like one word, even. As my father tried to pass her he cursed louder, with venom, and my mother crouched back shrieking. Her black hair stuck out stiff around her face.

I could see my mother's lips quivering. My aunt kept repeating: 'You can't be upsetting respectable people like this!'

'Begone, you ruffian!' my granny shouted. She was standing up, her spectacles awry. 'For shame! Let you get back where you came from!'

There was a lot of talk, My father stood in the doorway, breathing in hard short gasps. He wanted some tool and it couldn't be found.

23

'Look, Maggie,' he said in a high, shaking voice. 'I'm a hard-working man. And she has no respect for me. That *bitch*—'

'Don't listen to the dirty rotter!' my mother screamed. He made a move as though to strike her.

'Bitch!' she yelled at him. 'Bitch — bitch — bitch!'

My father cursed her. My mother retorted with the same curse — screaming it. Each time I felt my body freeze.

'A nice exhibition you're making, the pair of yous!' Maggie said fiercely. 'There's no call for such conduct. None whatsoever!'

'In the name of God, stop it,' Nana said.

He still stood, the full of the doorway, repeating that he was a good man and not one of them had any respect for him. His eyes were wild, his voice droned in a plaintive monotone. He put a large hand to his breast, repeating the same things, about his job and the way they were plotting against him. 'Then I come home and find my chisels hacked! Maggie, she lets them kids do what they like. If I go to chastise them I'm the worst in the world.'

At last Maggie got him out and quickly shut the door behind him. He went with a slow step past his carpenter's bench on the lobby, into the Far Room. There was no sound. My mother moved softly to the door and listened.

'The baby is in the bedroom. I'll stay there. Come on, Joe, bring Michael with you.'

She tiptoed out. Then I saw my brother Joe, who had been with her. He crept out fearfully with mother, gripping her hand.

After that my father stayed up half the night, hammering and sawing at his bench. I saw him as I went past timidly to bed. He was standing at his bench, a length of planed wood in his hand. There was a foam of shavings round him, and in the bluish air the smell of wood and stale tobacco smoke. I went past, staring. My father held the piece of wood between his hands and he was looking at it, breathing hard, his mouth shut tight.

The next morning, wakening, I knew he was in the room. Then I remembered, gladly, he'd soon be going out to work. He went, and I was free to move again.

'Get up, Michael,' my mother said. 'Your tea's poured out.'

She was sitting at the table with her back to me, cutting bread. Curled up at the far end of our bed Joe seemed still asleep.

'Yes, mother, I'm getting up now.'

I put my clothes on hurriedly and let my boots thump on the floor. Any noise was a relief, so doleful was the silence. At the table I avoided looking

24

at my mother and pretended to eat up the bread and butter hungrily. It would be better to seem quite at ease. It would only make it worse if there was any sign I was remembering.

Grafton Street, Dublin.

This Is Our Gate

There was a white envelope in the hall addressed to Maggie. Mother brought it up. Maggie had gone to her work in Browne & Nolan's Printers, so we had to wait for the lunch-hour when she would open the letter. She got the paper knife and was trembling with excitement as she read.

'We have a house,' she said, after a moment. 'This is the notification from North's.'

'I told you,' Nana said. 'Saint Anthony never lets me down — God is very good to us.'

'We're well away now,' Maggie said. She read the letter again slowly, with respect: '"The dwelling-house known as Roseville, Sandymount Avenue." I'll have to dash over for the key. I must fly,' she said, gulping her tea while holding her little finger well out from the bone-china cup, 'or I'll be late getting back to work after.'

Maggie had had her name down for a house since Christmas. After much prayer and patient waiting, at last, in summer, the prayers were being miraculously answered. Tomorrow, Saturday, they would be going and with joyful amazement I heard that I could go with them. It seemed too wonderful. I could only dare to hope it might come true.

'Saturday's flittin' short sittin',' my mother said in a despondent mood, but granny was happily packing a tea-chest.

'Maybe so,' she said, 'and maybe not. We'll only have to wait and see, as Mr Asquith says.'

I watched Nana wrapping newspaper around cups and plates and the grey china jug and putting them and a teapot in the wicker basket. It was a sign we really were going. The others would be left behind, but I felt only an eager excitement to be gone. To banish dreadful doubts I'd steal a glance now and again at the wicker basket, ready and waiting.

Early the next morning the basket was in granny's hand, she was wearing

26

her jet-bead cape and we were waiting for the tram. Its high step I climbed up by myself. The tram rushed so fast *ding-a-dong* that people on the pavement walking seemed stuck as we flipped past. Soon enough we had come to a sort of country place with grand houses and trees, and granny said 'We'll get off here.' I was handed down by the conductor. We were at the corner of a beautiful road with a curving, tree-topped wall and leafy, level shadows.

Granny took my hand in a tight grip and we walked along this road, on and on, and I kept asking anxiously 'Where is the house?' I think granny was anxious too, she snapped: 'Shut up!' She was looking and looking at each house till at last, near the end of the avenue, granny stopped at an olive-green gate. She peeped up and down the road, then at the name on the gate, and said in a low voice: 'This is the house.'

Then it happened — and unforgettable. Granny had her hand on top of the gate while I stood close beside her. She was gazing at the house, which for me was out of view because the gate was taller than myself. This gate was the colour of holly-leaves, and it had openwork panels quivering with light. The wrought-iron panels, dark green, duskily framed a cheerful shining which was like a loving, inviting smile. Peeping, I saw a softly shadowed garden which had the smell of morning in it, and above the gentle haze enfolding all was beaming down the tall, calm, silver sun. So high and so serene the sun shone that its light filled glowingly the morning-misted scene.

I stood rapt in wonder but the gate moved. Like a dark, obliterating cloud the shape of granny in her jet cape moved before me, up a tile-bordered path to the house. I followed with resentful, dragging steps till we came to the entrance, a glass porch. In here, while granny was opening the hall-door with her key, there was the perfume of geraniums like country dust. Above me were panes of coloured glass, deeps of blue and green and crimson. I stepped into this wondrous glow and saw its colours on my outheld hand.

'Where are you?' a hollow voice called. It was granny inside! I went into the hall, then into a room which was empty but for a large bare window, with its shape in sunlight on the floor. The chemical scent of my red toy engine was here, only stronger; the smell of new cream paint. Going on tiptoe to the window, I saw the garden rising outside, and upstairs I heard granny opening doors and walking about in the still house. She called me, and we gazed down at the garden from an upstairs window.

Granny said, then: 'We've seen the house, it's time we went home.'

In the tram going home I kept trying to swallow the pain in my throat.

27

People sitting opposite stared straight before them. Granny too had the stern, fixed look of people in a tram, but at last I couldn't bear but ask: 'Will we be going back?'

What relief, what joy to hear her say: 'Yes, yes! Of course!'

At home the sky looked dark, more like winter than summer. Evening came, but before that, all day long, granny, with my mother sometimes helping, had been putting things in boxes and tying things with cord. Later a man would come to take away the furniture.

By evening it had begun to rain but mother had me ready. I forget if I saw Joe and Meg before leaving —luckily *he* had not come home. Maggie took my hand and I went with her, dressed in my sailor suit with the brass buttons. Granny had gone on ahead and would be there already, in the house. How dark it had become! Even in the gloom I recognised with joy the lovely, curving corner of the avenue.

As we hurried along my aunt said there was lightning in the distance, we might see the bayonets of the soldiers in France flashing across the sea. I pictured the bayonets in darkness, all suddenly bright. We were passing a high wall and could see nothing but its granite grey.

Maggie had not yet seen the house. I told her I would show her where it was, and when we came to it I said: 'This is our gate.' Gently I touched the inset iron panels, which felt hard and knobby.

The furniture had only just arrived. Quickly granny answered the door, brought us into the kitchen where the gas was lit, and made the tea. Being then only five I had to go to bed soon after, on a mattress on the floor. I had a whole room to myself. It seemed strange to kneel beside a mattress on the floor. When I got into bed I realised how much alone I was, far from home. In the dark I listened to the storm and saw the tall, dim windows. Thunder shuddered as the windows stood out white.

Later they both came to the door to ask if I was frightened, but I wasn't. Granny and Maggie said: 'Goodnight. God bless.'

After we walked all the way to Mass and back on Sunday, they were busy in the kitchen cooking the dinner. It was cooked on a gas-stove — you put a penny in the meter, a match to the gas, and there it was! 'What a great invention,' granny said. Maggie was examining the built-in cupboards and she said that every room had an electric light you could switch on.

On Monday the house was empty but for me and granny. She was peeling potatoes in the kitchen. I could go out in the garden if I liked, she said, which seemed a daring thought. I stood on the crazy paving staring at the leaves, the grass, the stones. The garden was very wet, and all around there was that country garden smell, and there were hedges, and trees, and flowers, and a blackbird hopping. The leaves held glinting beads of light.

It was all right at first, then I felt lonely in the silence of the tall grass and the evergreens, and wished a friendly face would peep over the garden wall and say 'Hello!' Outside in the avenue I had seen other children playing. Maggie told me that they were better-class children so I couldn't play with them, but I had seen them.

There being nothing much to do, a great event that evening was when granny put on her jet-bead cape to go out shopping. I skipped along, delighting in the sun-struck evening shadows of Sandymount Green. You had to be sedate when going for a walk with Maggie, which took all the good out of it. With granny I could run ahead, she didn't mind.

We had been settled down a few days in the house when mother came to see it, and to see granny and me. I happened to be near the gate, which opened suddenly and there she was. She had a pile of parcels on the go-car with Meg sitting up in it as bold as brass, and Joe beside the go-car grinning. In a brown-paper bag was a present for me, a coloured picture book.

Mother kept raising her two hands in amazement and crying out how splendid it was, as granny showed her round the house. We trooped back to the kitchen. 'Well it's lovely, now lovely!' mother said. 'Ain't yous in luck — and so beautifully situated.'

She had brought a few bottles of stout, poured out in two glasses on the table. 'Well yous landed on your feet all right, yous are in town,' mother said. She handed me a cup with a small amount of stout in it, pale brown and beady. I went and got my beetle with the quivering elastic legs to let Joe see it. He began to cry for it and I had to scream at him to shut up. Mother said it was time they were going; it was getting late anyway. So we all went together as far as the tram.

The next day, around dinner-time, there was a knock. Granny jumped up eagerly, brushing specks of snuff off her black blouse. 'Pop along into the garden with your book,' she said. I wandered out to turn over the pages, quite pleased with the notion of myself in the garden with a book.

Shortly afterwards the door of the back porch clicked open and there appeared a gentleman wearing a new suit. You could see that he was a great reader, he was wearing glasses. He might come over to where I sat on a stone, and ask me about my book. Then he might put his hand on my head, I thought, and remark to granny what a clever boy I was. As granny stood beside him with her hands together the gentleman stared all around the garden but seemed not to see me sitting there. After he had taken a good look, both of them went in.

Maggie and granny were talking at tea-time, and I heard my granny saying that a gentleman had settled on the house, we would be going home tomorrow. 'Ah, well,' aunt Maggie said, 'it was too good to last.'

After tea we all went into the back garden, admiring it for the last time, pausing to stare up at the pale green globes amid the leaves of pear and apple trees. There was a cool breeze, granny had gone in, and as Maggie and I walked slowly to the house she murmured to herself: 'The shades of eve are falling fast. Another day near done.' Then she sighed her usual great sigh: 'Oh! Harry-ho!' My aunt often said she had feet like a doll, (size four they were, in stubby patent-leather shoes) but instead of smiling like a doll she had a sad expression now.

My Mother and Him

While we were away in Roseville there had been changes in the shop. Miss Carney had given the left-hand window and half the shop to a strange lady who did embroidery. She was an honourable, the Honourable Emily Lawless, a very suitable name, Maggie said, it being known that Miss Lawless wrote poems in favour of the Fenians.

That Monday when I brought down the rent Miss Carney beckoned me into the bonnet-room. It was behind the shop, with a side door onto the hallway and stairs. She put a bowl in my hands and said: 'Eat every bit of that.' It was a beautiful white pudding like flake rice, with nutmeg.

Sometimes on a Monday mother fine-combed my hair, she said, for nits. I had to kneel with my head bent over paper on a chair. The fine-comb reefing through my dull-gold curls brought gasps and tears, but it was worth it. I could hear tiny hard plops as lice fell, to crawl greyly in a sediment of dusty hairs.

Mother had many other jobs to think of. I could remember the warm feel of her hands gripping my legs when she held me out to ta. That was years ago, even Joe was able to ta on the pot by himself now. To us it seemed awful the way mother had to hold Meg over the pot, and say in a coaxing tone: 'Now do your peetney.' And: 'Ta, ta. Do your ta.' Unlike us Meg had only a small fat ridge between her legs, yet she could peetney all right. There'd be an awful stink in your nose from the brown ta, it had to be taken away under paper.

When Meg was about one my father had to go to Belfast for a boxing tournament. His going was a great relief; we were in raptures. I knew my father and mother were not fond of each other and we were always glad when he went out. He would be gone for two whole days, mother said.

How different it felt to be free and easy, sprawling on the floor, with *him* away! My mother lit the gas-jet: out bulbed the white light making

31

solid shadows. The fire was red, the kettle puffed and bubbled. Between two chairs I found an oblong shadow and curled snugly into it, as small as possible. Even my fingers and toes were inside the shadow-house. A step sounded unexpectedly, the door opened. It was him!

Mother was ready with a rush of talk and questions. She stood at the table bent slightly forward, cutting bread and excitedly talking, talking. My father threw his cap down on the sofa. He strode in heavily, his leather bag fell on the floor and he stood grinning.

'Well, missus, I didn't win, but I didn't lose. It was a draw. So I got half the purse.'

'I see you got a knock, mister, you got a bit of a knock.'

'Never seen such a crowd,' my father said ignoring this, sitting back from the fire. 'They had to turn people away, every seat in the stadium booked out.'

'Well now would you believe it?' mother said. 'Booked out.'

'There was a crowd up from Dublin in the train, standing room only there and back. Are you wetting a cup of tea, missus? There does be cadgers and trick-o'-the-loops of every kind in crowds like that. I had to be careful with the bit of money.'

In the Belfast digs he pushed his bed against the door, tied the prize-money in the tail of his shirt and lay awake all night. Now to mother's delight he put a few notes on the table. She said: 'Thanks, mister. That'll give us a little plentness.'

'We'll all go to Merrion next Saturday,' he said. 'It'll break the monotony.' It was a seaside place near Dublin on the Kingstown-Dalkey line. The tram finally stopped where a vision of rocks and sand and sea cut short the houses.

There was a white railway gate. We had to walk across the railway tracks. Behind a bit of a wall we found a strand with a few rocks, half worn away by all the people who had sat there, so we sat down.

In front of us heaved and gleamed the smooth sea, with the tide, my father said, nearly full in. It had a real salty, sea-weedy smell. It was a great place for cockle-pickers when the tide was out and the satiny pool-bright strand reached away to the horizon. Crowds of common people from the slums of Dublin congregated here, along the rocky foreshore, and made fires and boiled kettles of tea.

We made a small fire from bits of driftwood we collected, and we made a nice pot of tea and we had bread and butter. The real common way some of the children shouted was shocking. People were walking in the water, paddling, it was called. Mother said Joe and I could take off our shoes and

32

paddle, and even Meg paddled, screaming eagerly.

The water felt icy cold but after a while it was lovely, smooth and even, breathing slowly up, down, up and down. I faced away from the shore and went paddling on, then as the lapping sea came higher I began to wade.

I had to hold my pants up as the lazy wavy water deepened. All around me was the shining sea and keeping straight on, I waded out, out. I kept wading till my head rang from a slap on my right ear. I swayed around and there was my naked father towering over me. I saw his thing like a pale fat maggot half-hidden by the black hair of his belly. He shoved me on, gripping my arm tight and driving me before him towards where the others sat watching.

'He could have been drownded,' he told mother. My ear still ached from the blow but I knew I had done wrong.

I was old enough to know better, going on six. That winter mother took me to the barber. With a sickened feeling I realised that slowly but surely I was growing up. The time would surely come, one day, when I would be a man.

The barber put me kneeling in a padded chair. In the mirror I could see only my frightened face blooming up through a tent of spotted cloth. The old fellow kept humming to himself, a grey old barber with bocketty glasses. When he had finished snipping and sighing and humming I felt cold all round my head.

Luckily I could forget myself in some new happening or promised joy. The days were shortening and darker evenings made the street lamps bright. Already we could begin to count the week after long week till it would be Christmas again. It gave a preliminary feeling of excitement, and gazing from our window we imagined that the crowds going home in the dark must be as delighted as ourselves.

I suppose the change in the shop had to happen, but when Miss Carney went we all felt sorry. We never knew the reason, only that Miss Carney had left, and of course Miss Lawless had to give up her part of the shop as well. Promptly, then, Miss O'Leary came on the scene and had Miss Carney's name blotted out, and 'Miss O'Leary Ladies Wear' put over the shop with gold borders.

Miss O'Leary was a wiry little pink-faced lady from the heart of the country with grey hair trailing from under her hat. From the bonnet-room she kept pouncing in and out to the hall-door, to see and know everything.

On her very first day, as I was coming in with granny's snuff, a poor man arrived from the Deaf and Dumb Mendicity, and knocked. Miss O'Leary put her face right up to him, squeezing her eyes tight to see

33

better. He was begging, but he could only point to what was printed on the card.

'What's this? Deaf and dumb? Oh you're a dummy!'

Hissing with annoyance, Miss O'Leary banged the hall-door in his face.

My mother said one look at O'Leary was enough. 'Trust the country mugs — not long up but well up,' she said. 'Mark my words, that oul spit-fire's out for trouble. Well, she'll meet her match!'

Soon Miss O'Leary had a wooden hut built at the stair's end, to close off her basement and the shop side entrance. She still kept popping out to accost all comers, complaining that we banged the hall-door, or that we failed to bang it shut.

'I won't have muddy feet along my hall,' she would shout up the stairs. 'Nor people neither, tramping up and down my house!'

The toilet was uncomfortably near Miss O'Leary, at the top of a side flight up from the first landing. Being nearly six I could go to the toilet myself. Now I had to creep up like a mouse, fearing to be heard and seen and challenged. One day I found painted on the toilet door two scraggly, enormous letters. I asked mother what the letters were, and she said scorn-fully: 'Oh, it's just like her and her common ways — them letters are W.C. It means water closet; that's her way of saying "toilet". But sure the only toilet that one ever knew would be some bog-hole — or in behind a hedge!'

The scraggly W.C. came as an afterthought. Before this Miss O'Leary had been out in the street, painting our two stone pillars. They were in front of the arched gateway beside the house, through which in olden times a horse and carriage must have clattered into the cobbled yard behind. Now the iron gates looked old and closed and dark, but Miss O'Leary brightened the granite pillars by daubing them green, white and yellow — like two Irish flags.

'That O'Leary woman must be off her head,' Maggie said, coming in flustered at lunch-time. 'Tell Teazie (my mother) to take no notice of her whatsoever. *I* simply ignore her.'

The way the hall-door was guarded by Miss O'Leary made it an ordeal going out or coming in but you had to go out just the same. Joe and I could go together as far as the Duke's Lawn, or I might be sent by my father down to Moffey for the *Final Buff Mail*, which had all the latest horse-racing results. 'Tell him you want the full box.'

I was able to go for messages even to Lincoln Place, to the frosty-nosed chandler, Magrane, for our paraffin oil, or to Gogan's for Lemon's pure sweets for Nana. She would always share them, and I even went as far as

Denzille Street for fruit cake — its common name was 'gur-cake' — displayed in the window in long slabs.

On the left, in Denzille Street, was Lynch's, which was easily the best shop there. You'd have to stand real tall to examine what was crammed inside the high-up window, studs and hairpins, balloons, puzzles, mechanical wind-up toys Made in Germany, huge Christmas stockings. Hanging up in one corner, mysterious and special, there was a small grey metal toy called a Jew's harp. Something even better and gleaming caught my eye, though, lying close to the glass — a silvery, fat mouth-organ. Its curved silver side looked streaky-black; and its red line of tiny square holes, deeply black, held a richness of silent music. I vowed that that mouth-organ would be mine by Christmas.

They had coloured festoons hanging up in Findlater's when I went in for a quarter of rashers, a half-pound of margarine, and an empty box, please, if you have one. This was a better-class shop, so high class that the shop-men wore white coats, and they were always grinning and making jokes to one another. We always had butter ourselves. Margarine, mother said, was good enough for *him*, he'd never know the difference, but to make sure, the blue word *margarine* would be torn off and flame up in the fire.

After weeks of waiting I was given half-a-crown from the Christmas money and having rushed over to Lynch's, I brayed on my mouth-organ all the way home. Miss O'Leary, with her long-distance gimlet vision, had heard and seen all and was at the hall-door waiting. She made a grab to take it off me, but I whipped the mouth-organ behind my back. We stood face to face, Miss O'Leary hissing.

'Yous'll not make a bedlam of this house!' She made another unsuccessful grab. 'Scum and dirt, that's all yous are!' she panted. 'Get up out of my sight! Get up there now and quick about it!'

Once upstairs I savoured the magic of my mouth-organ: its weight, its glossy bulk, its hidden mystery. For me, with neither mind nor ear for music, the vibrations that filled the air were thrilling. The awful drone went on till I was hunted out of granny's room. Christmas jollity itself turned sour at the constant braying. 'Begone! And take that infernal thing with you!' Maggie said. Even in the far room I could find no peace — mother said: 'Shut up with that thing, or get out!'

Eventually, even to myself, the music seemed only a nuisance. I decided that comics and books were far more magic. In fact the nicest part of Christmas that year was my gift from Miss McCarthy, a big coloured picture-book about *Jack the Giant-Killer*. I begged Maggie to read out the story. She was after her tea, and had settled by the fire with her paper and a bar of Fry's cream chocolate.

'Ah, leave me alone,' Maggie grumbled. In her good moods she called me 'Coaxalorum', so I kept pushing the book against her, nudging her, till at last she began reading the story in an off-hand way. It kept getting better, more exciting, till she came to the terrible part where the Giant began to smell around, and to say in a thunderous mutter:

Fee, fi, fo, fum! I smell the blood of an Englishman!

Let him be dead or alive,

I'll have him for my supper!

At that point Maggie cut it short, in spite of my pleading. She could be hard as iron. 'No, you'd only have nightmares. We'll finish it some other time.'

Then she picked up her *Evening Herald:* 'Aw, Mazie, look at this!' It was a cartoon of a soldier in the trenches, reaching up to shake hands with a bright-faced little boy wearing a military cap lettered 1916. The smiling child said: 'Good luck, Tommy! Happy New Year!'

Maggie started to read out the usual dull grown-up stuff in her newspaper voice:

Lull in Verdun Battle — Enemy still held on Meuse heights.

Nothing important during last night.

Alleged capture of 17,000 French troops.

U-boat War — New campaign starts.

'Oh laws!' Maggie exclaimed. 'What next? — after them hospital ships and the *Lusitania*. Them Germans must be monsters.'

'God help all them poor sailors,' granny said quietly. Munching her choc-bar Maggie read on:

Brandenburgers Trapped — Splendid Dash by French Infantry.

Fighting at Donaumont.

Press Association War Special Paris Tuesday Delayed.

'"Delayed,"' Maggie said. 'Note that — "delayed." God alone knows what them poor fellows are going through.' She read on to see:

Our soldiers retook Donaumont — responding to the call of their leader who knew his men well, having already led them several times to victory.

'Famine amongst Bulgarians,' Maggie read. 'Still and all, that's a terrible thing, a living death. They still have Our Gallery of Heroes, Irishmen who have Fought and Bled for Us — will you look at the poor fellows' photos, all massacreed! May God have mercy on them.'

'Amen,' granny said. She peered over. 'What's that about Girl's Action? Up there on the right.'

Maggie looked, saw it, read with new attention:

Girl's Action for Alleged Breach — Matchmaking in Dublin.

Defendant still willing to marry.

Aunt's alleged interference.

'There's a brazen huzzy — making a proper show of herself,' Maggie said. 'According to the man in the case, it was a made match anyway. It says here. "Giving evidence on his own behalf, defendant said:

I was approached by Simon Benjamin of Lombard Street who suggested that I should get married, and that *he knew a nice girl*.

'Fancy that now — he knew a nice girl,' Maggie said scornfully. 'Defendant went on: "I knew the girl myself, having seen her on several occasions when visiting the neighbourhood on business. I considered her a decent, respectable girl and was prepared to accept her as my wife."

'Well the cheek of that! And I see here,' Maggie went on, 'that it turns out the man was nothing but a pedlar selling from door to door. She'd be better off single, if you ask me.'

Granny, straightening her spectacles, was peering again.

'What's that about Turkish Delight?'

'I thought it meant sweets,' Maggie said. 'No it isn't an ad, only "Turkish Delight at the Allies' evacuation of Gallipoli." Sure the paper is full of ads, though: "Tiz for aching, sore, tired feet." Too true, it's the way I feel myself.'

Granny smiled: 'I'd love to dance, but O my feet!'

'And I meant to renew the water of them flowers.'

'I'll do it, Maggie.'

I went to the altar and onto the dark landing outside, carrying the little vase of winter roses. The sink was out here, and the tap. I took from the vase the frail flowers and evergreens and let the water flow. Someone was coming up the stairs. My father's voice called in the dark: 'Who's that?'

'It's me — Michael.'

'Oh, Mick is it.' He came up to the landing and paused. In the dark I could smell tobacco as he said in a low, confiding tone: "I don't want to make a shoddy job of it — that box I told you I'd make for you. I could use nails or screws, but you need to dovetail and round off to do it right. Come here a minute Mick, I'll show you.'

He strode along the unlit lobby — we had no gas-jet there — and came back from the far room carrying the tall brass oil-lamp.

'Mick!' He put the lamp on the bench and pointed to the floor. 'Will you pick up that wedge?'

I picked it from among the shavings. My father took the small triangle in his hand. I stood fingering the vase of flowers.

'This is what they call a wedge,' he said, watching me keenly. I felt dismayed. I hated shavings, and saws, and carpentry.

'I know,' I said sullenly.

My father stared at me. The vertical lines in his dark face seemed to deepen.

'Don't say you know. You don't know — I'm telling you. If you knew already, would I have to tell you?'

He pushed the wedge forward to steady an upright of wood.

'See that?'

'Yes.'

My father stooped his wrinkled forehead towards me. His voice was low but firm, insistent. 'Now that holds the wood in its place. Understand?'

'Yes, I know.'

'Don't say you know!' he retorted. 'Say you understand. How can you know till you're told?'

'I understand, Mister.'

He grew calm again.

'Now look at this, Mick.' His blunt thumb moved along the smooth-grained wood. 'This is what they call a camber, do you get me? This is what they call a camber.'

'Yes.'

After leaving the vase back with Maggie I returned to the bench. No doubt he expected me to be a carpenter some day. The scent of shavings, the harsh tobacco smell and all the tools and nails filled me with loathing, but my father kept on explaining patiently. He told me that my tools must always be kept sharp, a good workman is known by his tools.

'That's what *she* doesn't seem to realise,' he went on, bending down to me and speaking in low, earnest tones. 'She's careless, Mick. She seems to have no intellect at all. Me tools are thrown anywhere, and they get hacked, and then —'

'Michael!' My mother opened the door. It was dark inside, the gas-mantle must have broken. 'Come here, I want you.'

'Can't you let him alone?' my father said, turning his head. 'If he remains here I can learn him something.' He lowered his voice again. 'There's no harm in knowing, do you get me? Here.' He picked up a plane. 'When you want to get the blade of your plane plumb, take a hammer and give it a few taps, like that.' He tapped one end of the plane. 'That drives the blade in further.' He tapped the other end. 'And that drives it back, see?'

Mother came to the door again, and said: 'There's a cup of tea wet,

38

Mister.' She spoke in a mild, easy way and he went in at once, stopping only to repeat his promise to make me a box of my own, with lock and key.

It was late. Meg and Joe were in bed, and when I'd had my cup of tea I went to bed too. The oil-lamp gleamed on the mantel. I felt wide awake, thinking of my box-to-be, and Jack the Giant-Killer.

I suppose mother will go into the bedroom now, I thought. Then he will sit there alone. Then after a while he will get up, and throw the end of his cigarette in the fire before he turns down the lamp. Then his loud footfalls, the door closing.

But no. My mother and father stayed sitting at the fire. I could hear my brother snoring. He seemed to be dreaming, mumbling in his sleep. I saw my mother leaning towards my father, whispering something. He bent his head nearer to listen. He asked some question, in a gentle tone. So that is what they mean, I thought. It is another child. In the morning, with a sort of guilty feeling, I remembered still the wonder that I knew.

College Green in the early 1900s, showing Trinity College and, on the left, the Bank of Ireland, once Grattan's Parliament.

Mrs Howard ('The Little Woman'), and aunt Maggie.

Dalkey People
Are
Themselves

It was a freezing day with feathers of snow falling. In the dusk of the evening Joe and I went out to play. There were small amounts of snow shimmering here and there, not enough to fire snowballs. I could see the street lights, a straight line of them along Merrion Square and as far as Mount Street.

It was exciting, the strangeness of being out so late on snowy ground. Moffey was there calling 'Herrildy-Mail!' A curious thing, then — we seemed to smell it out. We crossed the road to Merrion Square and there it was, a perfect, long slide big boys had made on the frozen footpath.

Joe gave a whoop of delight. He was right. We were able to go sailing along the slide, skimming along to turn smoothly, then after a quick little run glide all the way back. A glorious feeling like flying, and as you swept along the row of gold lights overhead went up, up like a blazing rod into the blue-black sky.

Crouched down, feet straddled sideways, effortlessly gliding I could see the surface of the gleaming icy slide, streaks of silvery-black like my mouth-organ. All merged as a wonder of wonders — the rod-like lights, the deeps of silver-black, the powerful forward-flowing glide —

'Get to hell home outa that!' a man shouted. 'Yous an' your skatin' — all the same if someone breaks their bloody neck!' Another old man stood and shook his fist at us, we had to clear off home.

Soon enough the days took on the cold brightness of wind-swept March. We were deep in the dreary season known as Lent, a time when you'd feel half-ashamed of eating a few sweets. But my granny, Nana, still sent me down for her snuff.

'It must be the war,' Maggie said. 'People don't fast the way they did when I was small. We had black tea and dry bread.'

'Or bread and dripping instead of butter,' granny said.

41

'I used to live for *Nuggets*,' Maggie said, 'but for the whole seven weeks we never even took a peep. Laws, when I think of it! Week after week we put *Nuggets* away, under the mattress. When Lent was over — boys O boys! It was heaven open to sinners; we could read and suck sweets till the cows came home.'

My father called it Length, a good description.

'Don't talk to me about Length,' he'd say. 'It's easy for the clergy to give up meat and tell the rest of us to starve ourselves. They can enjoy their smoked salmon. I'd give up meat any day if I had salmon — Length or no Length!'

My father pushed Lent to one side, he seemed to be betting on horses worse than ever. Street-betting was illegal, but he used to say: 'Put a few bar on for me each way, with Uno Mac.'

That meant going over to Denzille Street and down an alley where Uno Mac always stood between twelve and one o'clock. Mother would send me running down to him, a skinny man in a raincoat with a cigarette in his mouth, writing his dockets.

'He does have a kid on the look-out,' mother said. 'At the first sign of a bobby he's over the wall.'

The following day Uno would be back in his usual place to take bets and pay out on winning dockets, printed green-white-yellow *Uno Mac*.

Mother said in Lynch's one day she might buy me a hoop for Easter. I had seen them, big wooden hoops hanging up near the ceiling. From that moment I wanted nothing but a hoop and nearly cried for one. 'Maybe next week,' mother said, and for the time being she bought me a celluloid egg.

Well, that was a puzzle. The glass-like egg was a perfect egg shape, and inside it was a fluffy yellow chick. Nobody could say how the chicken got inside the egg. It was amazing.

There would be a holiday next week, Maggie said, so she would spend the Sunday and Monday in Dalkey — and she would take me with her in the train! This was better than anything. There had often been talk about far-away Dalkey, the Coliemore (the Big Harbour), and the sea. Aunt Bessie lived there, and her sister, the Little Woman, Mrs Howard. They were sisters of my granny that aunt Maggie used to visit, but this would be the first time she had taken me.

I was so happy I even drank my Saturday dose of senna tea without making a face. It was quite sickening but it was medicine so you had to take it — unlike seed cake. Anyone that hated seed-cake could have bread and jam instead, in granny's room.

As usual Maggie was fit to be tied getting ready, and getting me ready, to go out on Sunday morning. After Mass we were to get straight onto the train at Westland Row. In the meantime there was all this fuss.

'Turn round at once!' My aunt's glum, flushed face came nearer as she re-did the bow under my chin and pulled my coat with a jerk to button it. Doing this she caught sight of my knees and exclaimed: 'Sweet Lord! Them knees — get your mother to wash them this minute! Comb that awful quiff again, and brush them boots!'

Excitement surged as I feverishly polished my boots. Maggie had tightened them up with a button-hook and now her voice came raging through her open door.

'We couldn't have better luck!' Maggie fumed. 'There's me lavender gloves gone again — I'll fly out of this bedlam stark frantic!'

There went the chapel bell; we were in good time after all. Maggie looked very stand-offish in her Sunday clothes with the white frilly blouse. By now she was wearing her lavender gloves, and also the ear-tips of eau-de-Cologne she always put on visiting.

After Mass we made a mad rush for the railway station. It was a dark hollow kind of glasshouse. Our carriage brightened as the train chuffed from the station and the sun struck in. Maggie sat with a very solemn face looking straight before her, never at other people in our carriage. We sat in opposite corners. Once or twice she nodded to me with a strained, wan smile, directing my gaze to the sea, or cattle grazing.

It was a long, long journey, about eight miles in all. Suddenly Maggie looked excited. 'Good old Dalkey!' she exclaimed out loud, forgetting herself at sight of the familiar station with its little semi-circle of white railings moving slowly to a stop.

Maggie had different relations in this place, cousins named Roe, and the Byrnes, and Mog Byrne who lived in Ballybrack. This is the real country, I thought with awe, as we went along a quiet sunlit road.

'The Roes live there,' Maggie said, 'in them houses where the eagle is.' I looked in the direction of the stone eagle, open-mouthed, gazing back over my shoulder. 'Don't stare!' my aunt said quietly. 'You couldn't look sideways here,' she added in a whisper, 'without everybody knowing it. Now I want to show you a grand old man, he's down along this road. He was out, sitting in the sun when I brought the Mazie along yesterday. A regular mane of silver hair he has, he does be out in the garden at about this time.'

'Is granny staying with aunt Bessie?'

'Not-a-tall! She's with the Little Woman. Bessie is bound to be wild, but sure she'll get over it. Don't let on you're lookin' — there he is now.'

As we passed I got a sideways glimpse of the old man at his door. In the noonday light his cheeks were red, his head and beard like snow. 'Eighty if he's a day,' my aunt said.

'The Dalkey people are themselves. They're independent, and they have their own way of doing things; woe betide you if you cross them! But they have the devil's own curiosity,' Maggie said, as we hurried on. 'You couldn't put your nose outside the door but you'd be noticed and commented on!'

We had come from the trim little station past shops and houses, I saw Castle Avenue, named after Archbold Castle, then turning several corners we reached a downward-sloping road which led to the harbour, the Coliemore. I remember coming to the low, fat, whitewashed wall of a narrow, steep-down lane. We went down, and the first cottage, right beside the wall, was Bessie's. These cottages had been built by Captain Archbold the great-grandfather, my aunt often remarked.

Carefully passing Bessie's cottage we turned in at the Little Woman's to see granny first. She was sitting in the sunshine with a plaid shawl round her, beaming at the sight of us. The Little Woman popped out blazing with gold and ebony rings, and earrings, and Maggie said we'd soon be back but take the Mazie in, she'd get her death sitting out there.

'But my God, surely you'll come in for a cup of tea!' Mrs Howard said, all excitement. A kind of war was going on between herself and Bessie, on whom the Little Woman had put a curse that Bessie would die first. 'Ah-ha, see that now,' Bessie cried, for all the cottages to hear. 'Well, while I'll be wakin' you'll be quakin'!'

With all this coolness going on, Maggie couldn't delay, but she said we'd be staying the two days anyway.

I felt nervous going into Bessie's. There was a tiny garden, then a long dark passage, very dark after the sunlight, then the kitchen with a gleaming range and a bottled, full-rigged ship on the high window-sill. Aunt Bessie was like Nana in appearance, only she was hard. She kept hens in the back yard.

A fisherman from the Coliemore had come before us bringing crabs and lobsters, and I saw aunt Bessie boiling them alive. She said that one time a crab nearly took the thumb off her. I was glad. I sat looking and listening, mouth open, my legs dangling from the chair. Aunt Bessie looked at me and said: 'Why don't you go out in the garden?' I felt too shy to move. It was nice being there, with the soft mournful sound of the women's voices and the rustling of uncle Joe's canaries in the breeding cage.

There was no sign of uncle Joe, or the lodger, Mr Sheen. Of course Mr Sheen had a room of his own. He was a Jewman and kept himself to himself, and Bessie said he was a quiet poor man.

When it got dark that evening, after tea, my aunt said: 'What on earth is wrong with you?' I knew very well. I wanted to ta, but couldn't bring myself to admit it, or say such a terrible word. I could only keep sobbing to myself, and saying that I wanted to go home. There was nothing for it but to take me — which meant taking Nana as well.

Maggie was annoyed with me even the next day. Then she cooled down a bit, saying that perhaps it was all for the best with the crowds that would be travelling this Easter Monday, so prone to accidents — one of the Cross Days, like Whit. She said we might as well go out early, as far as Stephen's Green. It was exactly the chance I needed to try my new hoop. Thanks to mother, it had been waiting for me in the Far Room beside the sofa, with a special little stick to drive it.

The wooden hoop was nearly as tall as myself and it had square edges all the way round. A great hoop, which I was bringing to Stephen's Green with my granny and Maggie. I had to hold it high, steering carefully down, down, flight after flight of stairway corners. Out on the footpath I could give my hoop a smack to see it driving on, perfectly straight and upright at great speed.

Ignoring Maggie's cries I ran ahead, bowling my hoop, though it wobbled near Moffey's and fell over, wobbled again at the Duke's Lawn. Maggie ran after me and gripped my free hand, and with me in the middle, much mortified, the three of us walked on sedately.

War Comes to
Dublin

In Stephen's Green, at any rate, I'd be free to run and bowl away just as I pleased. Meanwhile there was this being held by the hand as we turned into Merrion Row. The Green was in sight at last, but we'd have to cross the road, walk up to the corner and cross again.

'Always look both ways before you cross,' Maggie said, but there was no sign of motor cars. There was a peculiar stillness as we neared the corner. Here a few people were standing, staring across in amazement at the shut gates of the Green.

On this perfect circle, my hoop, all my hopes of a glad sunny morning were centred. On the smooth walks of the Green how swiftly I'd speed, driving my hoop on its oval, slim shadow! But something was wrong. The space between the corner of Merrion Row and the Green looked different, oddly vast. It was a deserted space. We realised that the gates of Stephen's Green were locked, and a wall of sandbags had been piled against them.

A few men, like figures on a distant stage, stood staring from behind the bars.

'Go home!' one of them shouted. He was waving at us, and shouted again: 'Go home or I fire!'

This fellow came out in front of the gates with a revolver in his hand. For a moment I could only gape, not even feeling annoyed. The man had a startling appearance. He was wearing a leopard skin like the big drummer in a band. He waved his gun at us again, threateningly: 'Clear away home!'

The four or five people near us were just as amazed as ourselves. Like us they had wanted to go into the Green — and here we were, stopped! It was natural to feel angry, but the big people seemed more excited than angry. They had clustered together and were all talking at once in low tones.

'What's up?' Maggie said, going over. 'What's the matter?'

Nobody seemed to know. One man said, staring across at the shut gates: 'There's going to be trouble.'

Maggie grabbed my hand and said, 'Come on, Mazie, we'd better be going home.' It was exciting and strange; we turned away reluctantly. As we moved on we met groups of people all eager and astonished, all talk and questions. Someone pointed along the street. There was a tram there, overturned. Rumours were flying that the Irish Volunteers had marched into Sackville Street, there would be a war.

When we got home Maggie opened up the bottom sash of her window and leaned out, gazing left and right. 'The city is like a desert,' she said, 'not a soul on the streets,' but I knew them furry fellows were in Stephen's Green. I got my toy revolver and ran to the window. Maggie pulled me back. 'I want to shoot them furry fellows!' I shouted, but she pushed me from the window. 'Do you want us all to get killed?'

We were all there at home as the holiday Monday worn on, dull and boring. That evening my father said he'd ramble over for a game of housey-housey, but he came back soon. 'I seen a tram on its side,' he told us (we had seen it already). 'There's a horse was shot dead near the college, and they have King Street barricaded.'

Maggie said all this trouble was caused by the Irish Volunteers. Nobody knew exactly who they were or what they were up to. 'A lot of hotheads,' granny said, 'that's what they are, hotheads and firebrands.'

Nobody in our family took an interest in politics, except maybe my aunt. If Maggie was pro anything I would say she was pro-British, reading out about the doings of the Royal Family. But she also knew about the Volunteers; in fact she had a photo of one of their leaders dressed in military uniform. She admired him because he was handsome and was named O'Reilly — her own name was Maggie O'Reilly. Only he named himself in Irish 'The O'Rahilly', which meant he was chieftain of all the O'Reilly clan.

At either side of our windows there were tall, narrow shutters which opened out as hinged panels. These were shut and barred. As darkness fell you could nearly feel the silence over the city. I went to bed with no notion of sleeping. Later, in total darkness, I lay listening to a mysterious noise down in the street, and it went on and on — the measured stroke, stroke, stroke of marching feet. Was it the Volunteers — or what?

Now in the darkness rang out the crackle of shooting, far and near. I knew about the war in the papers Maggie read, the fighting on the Western Front, rifle and mortar fire and bayonet charges. This marching and the banging of guns was all part of the war, it seemed, come nearer.

The next morning we peeped from our high-up windows at a line of soldiers on the opposite side. They were at our side too — all the way along Clare Street and Merrion Square, into the distance. The soldiers were suddenly there, ranged along both sides of our street holding their squat, sloped rifles at the ready.

It was like a dream that went on, all the time more bewildering. Of course nobody could go to work. The fact that my father was there, at home, didn't seem to matter because he was only ordinary compared with a drama like this. He would sometimes take a quick peep through the curtains.

Maggie wondered if she could slip out to get milk and bread. I came beside her in the hall, saw the door swing open and the soldier outside with his leather-strapped rifle. He had a funny way of talking, not like us.

The soldier said in a grand voice that Maggie could go out if she wanted to, at her own risk. He was keeping a sharp look-out. 'Hit's the snipers on the roofs,' he said. "It and run, that's their mottaew.' Maggie was raging, because 'hit and run' sounded so cowardly.

'You can't deny that they're brave men,' she said indignantly. 'Whatever else!'

'They're barmy,' the soldier said. 'That's wot *they* are.'

Waving her milk-jug, remembering her namesake hero, Maggie retorted: 'I don't care what you say. The O'Rahilly is a splendid man, and a real gentleman.'

Later, when granny was told about this it upset her. 'You and your O'Rahilly! You'll have them raiding the place next. And if they found that photo —'

'Well they won't!' Maggie put the photo down inside her blouse.

'All the same,' she went on, 'you'd really pity some of them poor Tommies. Sure they're only boys. There was one in the dairy drinking a glass of milk, and sis he, "Crikey," sis he, "it's werse than Flawnders!"'

Some of the people opposite — the quality — stood at their doors and chatted with the soldiers. They even brought out tea and sandwiches to them, which Maggie said was Irish hospitality.

The sky greyed over and all afternoon the rain pattered, dimpling the shiny pavements. We knew by now that there were Irish Volunteers barricaded in the Post Office in Sackville Street. We heard — which seemed a hard and brutal thing — that they had shot down looters thieving from shops. Also that crowds had gathered to watch the big shop, Lawrence's, go up in flames. There had come a lull in the shooting, but it only made the interval more tense as we waited for what must happen next.

Maggie said it was a good thing, anyway, that Miss O'Leary was not in evidence. She had gone home to the country for Easter, and with luck would be unable to get back.

Late that night, when I had gone to bed, we heard the thunder of big guns. By Wednesday morning the war had really started. The city seemed to shake. The terrible noise went on, sometimes wavering, then suddenly strong and intense: the yap-yap-yap of machine-guns, the crack of rifle-fire, the shuddering crump of artillery.

For a house-bound child of six it would be hard to imagine a more thrilling or marvellous experience. The way at night they would shout: 'Put out that light!' Soldiers on horseback clattering along — the cavalry — had been shot down in Sackville Street. When I peered out a Tommy opposite stared up at me from under his cap's peak, before his gaze went roving on along the rooftops.

On Thursday night the Far Room was in darkness. We knew that a great battle was being fought across the city. Pressing close against the window we could see the left side of Lincoln Place and Fanning's pub. High up, the ornamental roof of this building stood out in silhouette against a bright red sky.

We were beginning to feel sad, to feel a kind of sympathy for the Irish Volunteers. They were foolish men — hotheads all right, but they were fighting a losing battle now. You couldn't but feel sorry for them, even feel a sneaking pride.

Saddest of any news for Maggie was that The O'Rahilly was dead. He had been shot in Moore Lane, off Moore Street; she stood at the window and muttered a prayer for his soul. 'The whole of Dublin will be levelled,' she said. 'God have mercy on them — Jesus, Mary and Joseph protect them!'

The Volunteers in the GPO were holding out, though by this time the building and most of Sackville Street was blazing. Still the big guns pounded and the rifles cracked. Then all of a sudden it was finished. Quiet had spread over the city by Saturday evening, a great stillness. They had at last laid down their arms, a soldier said.

I remember being taken for a walk the next day by my father. We saw the tram on its side again, shop-windows broken by looters, bullet-marks in walls. We came to Westmoreland Street, and saw beyond it the piles of blackened rubble and the sky, an open space that showed the backs of houses in streets far away.

The walls that stood in Sackville Street looked ragged, as if my story

49

book giant had lumbered along punching holes in them with his fist. Where the roads and pavements had been level people were climbing and stumbling, and standing to stare. From the acrid-smelling ruins a plume of smoke was here and there still rising.

Carlisle (now O'Connell) Bridge and Eden Quay, Dublin.

Wonderland
and
Cumberland

When summer came I used to play in the Duke's Lawn. Around this little park grey buildings brooded: the Museum, the College of Science, the National Gallery. In the middle of the Lawn sat a large green-tinted lady, Queen Victoria, around whose monument I played with Sailor Hat.

I never deliberately met Sailor Hat, he was just there. He had a fragile, freckled face and he wore glasses. He was able to read, and this fact stabbed me with envy. To salve hurt pride I showed Sailor Hat my *Jack the Giant-Killer*, pretending I had read it. This was a lie. I was in the habit of telling barefaced lies and half believed them myself.

As the months went by a group of us played together, mostly running-around games like Tipping Tig and Relieve-ee-o. It was a sober enough setting for childhood joys. I think of people passing then, long dead no doubt, who glanced through the railings at our small figures running, and heard the childish voices calling distantly: 'All in, all in!'

By then we were going boldly into the tomb-like precincts of the School of Art. The grey walls rose to an impressive height, stone steps led down to granite depths, our voices echoed.

Despite all this adventure the evenings went on as before. I would be sitting in my little chair in Nana's room while Maggie's voice mourned on and on, reading the *Mail* or the *Herald*, reading a book by Zane Grey. The evenings grew darker. Winter came with sleet and snow and warm, gay Christmas; then one day in the increasing brightness certain trees in the Square were green with buds, and spring had come.

Then came a shock, something that fully justified my dread of growing old. The one who caused it was Mog Byrne of Ballybrack. She had a small garden sloping down to her neat, small house; she herself being a tall and narrow, bony lady with a high-pitched voice. She advised Maggie it was time — and past the time — for me to go to school!

On Monday I had a new school-bag with my lunch in it. The school was near our pawn-office, behind the Sisters of Mercy Convent. Mother knocked with her fist on the wooden door, and as we waited she put on a serious, cross face. A nun opened the door. The dusk inside showed up her stiff, white head-dress.

They just said a few words, then the nun smiled and nodded, that would be all right, and she took my hand. I looked back at my mother with her bent fingers, raised, waving bye-bye.

Next, in a room full of children, I sat watching another nun's back. A black hooded back. She began writing in chalk, then pointed her cane at each letter, *A, B, C, D.* We had to say it after her together, this was learning how to read.

Up in a corner hung a small, oily red lamp. The light was floating. Coldly it flickered up and down, big and small, in its glass bowl. It seemed to be swimming like a fish.

'Bee, See, Gee...' There were so many letters, all the letters of the alphabet. I knew they were too many for me, I'd never learn how to read. Ages later when a bell rang I still felt heavy-hearted. The boys all stood up and we marched into the yard. I had my school-bag on, it was time to eat my bread-and-butter lunch. I stood near a wall and other boys, eating their lunches too, stood watching me.

'What's your name?' a boy asked.

I told him.

'Where do you live?'

More of them crowded forward, asking where I lived. I decided to ignore them and simply stood eating my lunch. They pushed me back against the wall. My bread and butter fell. I felt enraged, and gave a savage growl.

Instantly a boy cried: 'Bulldog!' The others took it up with a delighted roar: 'Bulldog! Bulldog! Do the Bulldog!'

A young nun came towards us. They all darted away.

'Go and sit in the class-room!' the nun said sharply.

'Thank you, Sister.'

In the school-room I was alone. I could really look at the desks and the blackboard. The sweetly-sour smell of bread and school-bags filled the air. I began to feel uneasy, then frightened. Long ago I'd had that silly feeling of dismay at being Tiger Tim. My present dismay was much the same but it went deeper. This was not imaginary, they had called me — shouted with hatred and venom — 'Bulldog!'

Suddenly the nun of the class was looking down at me.

'What are you doing here?'

'What— I have a headache, Sister.'

She smartly boxed my ear.

'Don't tell me lies! Go back into the playground at once!'

I scowled at her, and went out to be met by shouts of 'Bulldog! Bulldog!' It was frightening the way they crowded round, pushing me back and forth. One of the bigger boys turned on them, 'Stop it.' Then he said to me, reasonably, 'Go on, do it. Go on, just this once.'

I growled. They wanted more, but the bell rang.

As soon as we got out I hurried to my waiting mother, and we went home with a gang of boys behind us calling 'Bulldog!' It was better to ignore them, we agreed, and the shouts would fade away. I was glad when she stopped coming. Joe came to the school now and I was big enough to take him home. Once beyond range of the other children with their chant of 'Bulldog!' Joe and I would chase each other, playing along the streets.

Joe was nearly six, I over seven. Compared with his pretty, laughing face and golden curls I was dark-haired and morose. I hated school, living only for the evenings when my aunt would go on reading from the place she had left off the previous night.

Maggie was able to get brand-new novels from her friend, Miss McCarthy in the paper-shop. It was a welcoming shop with coloured comics on the counter. If I got a penny I'd go down at once and buy some comic.

One day Miss McCarthy asked me: 'Have you read *Wonderland Weekly?*' She must have liked it herself, to say that. She was a nice dumpy lady, a bit like my aunt. She had rimless glasses, dark brown eyes, and a straight nose.

This *Wonderland Weekly* became a milestone in my life. I could hardly wait for it from Saturday to Saturday. The part I liked best was a follow-up story, 'The Adventures of the Little Brown Man', which Maggie read to me. The Little Brown Man was a magic sort of person, yet gentle and kind, and you felt for him in all his troubles. He only used his magic when he really had to, against his evil enemies.

The promise of being further informed of the Little Brown Man's adventures kept me good all the week. Every morning I obediently knelt and said my prayers for Nana, in front of the altar. When I set out for school she would be in bed still, sitting up against the pillows. Each evening, too, before I went in to bed I had to say more prayers. Our Lord's statue looked down at me calmly, tinged by the red light, his hands held out to me.

One evening Maggie said that I seemed to be making no progress at the convent school, so it would be a good idea to send me to the Brothers. I was getting too big for the nuns' school anyway, she told my mother, and the Christian Brothers were a splendid body of men. They turned out the best scholars in Ireland.

The entrance to the Christian Brothers' school was in Cumberland Street. It was the very opposite of Wonderland. The drab frontage was criss-crossed by iron stairs and braided with barred windows. A wind-swept corridor went through the building into the school yard. A door on the left of the open hall-door gave entry to my class — First.

The Brother in charge here, like all the Christian Brothers, wore a long black skirt and a broad cloth belt, folded over to swing at his side like a tail. Under the skirt were broad, black, polished shoes or boots. The walls were dark and blank, the windows high. We sat staring up at the ginger-headed Brother, who kept talking in a grumbling, loud voice. Under cover of our desk the boy beside me pinched my leg. 'Do the Bulldog,' he muttered, not moving his lips. 'G'wan. Do the Bulldog.'

Of course I wouldn't, so he pinched me again. I turned on him, scowling. Seeing this the Brother strode over gripping a thick, stiff black leather. He wagged the strap impatiently, expecting me to 'hold out'.

'But he pinched me!'

The Brother wagged his strap more urgently, I could only hold out my hand, palm up. The strap exploded in needle-sharp smacks. Quickly I squeezed the numbed hands under either arm while my grinning class-mate pinched me again.

In the yard at lunch-time boys gathered round me with genuine interest. Somehow the word had spread that I could growl and bark. Politely, I was asked to 'Do the Bulldog'. They insisted so much I began to feel flattered. 'Very well. I'll do it.'

Now I was firmly branded 'Bulldog'. There was no escape. Everything about the school was hateful, and after a week of misery I decided to mitch. There was a real bad lot called Cecil Sweeny — the chemist's son — who could smoke cigarettes and curse and tell dirty stories. I mitched with him and a fellow called Heffernan, who was really only a part-time mitcher.

I was eight years old, and ready to be every bit as bad as Cecil. We simply converged without comment and made our headquarters a lane nearly opposite the Protestant Hall in Merrion Street. We had a street-chant ready for any unfortunate 'Proddy' boys or girls we might spot around Merrion Hall:

'Proddy-woddy on the wall,
Half a loaf will do you all!'

After a few days of mitching there was every chance that Monday morning would mean back to school — if I was found out. This was a worrying fear. Also I felt depressed that I was over eight, and couldn't even read! Yet I made my way to the lane again on Saturday morning, glumly picking my way across joinings in the pavement to avoid bad luck.

Aladdin's Lane

The cobbled lane showed a sunny view of back doors, garage gates and dustbins. A carter, harnessing his horse, threw me a nod. On a higher level beyond the carter I could see the peak of Cecil Sweeny's big cap and part of his forehead, cut across by the edge of the flat roof he was sitting on. A sloped wire rope fixed to a telegraph pole made the ascent easy. The flat roof felt warm in the sun. Cecil was dozing, but hearing me arrive he opened his pale eyes. and closed them in recognition. We were never effusive.

Beside where we sat, or lay sunning ourselves, there was a grimy curve-topped window. It was the upper back window of an auctioneer's premises, a vast cave-like shop full of shadowy treasures.

I forget which of us thought of it first, but Cecil and I had agreed that Saturday would be a suitable day to force open the window and select a few things to take home. When Heffernan arrived later we went over the details. Cecil by now had got the window loose, but we would have to wait for further action till the afternoon when the lane would be free of snoopers.

Feeling restless we climbed off the roof, and by a happy chance as I was sliding down the wire I noticed a mouse near the wall. The second my feet touched ground I stooped and cupped my hands around him. The mouse was ours! Heffernan went searching for a piece of string which we patiently tied to his tail.

After some argument we agreed what to do with the mouse. He deserved a bit of a run in the sunshine. There was a stone ledge outside several shops in Merrion Street and here we sprawled, chins propped on our hands, to watch the mouse run to and fro. His pointed nose kept quivering towards the step leading to Gogan's sweet-shop. He was making for a hole under the step. It was fun to see him scurry half-way in, then

56

pull him all the way back for his run in the sun.

We were immersed in the spectacle of the mouse's frantic attempts to get away. A loud, horrified exclamation from behind made us look up with startled expressions. It was a lady who wanted us to let the mouse go free.

'But we caught him!' Cecil cried indignantly. 'He's ours!' Cecil had more spunk than Heffernan and me put together. Out came the lady's hand, holding a shilling. She said, in a tone that made the cord I held seem like a rope: 'You can have the shilling for giving that poor little creature its freedom.'

After spending the shilling we went back to our roof with three bars of chocolate and cigarettes. Cecil had matches, so we dawdled there eating and smoking till it was time to go home. The tobacco left a cloying taste which somehow added to the excitement I felt in thinking of our plan.

As I was going uncertainly into the far room I saw the bedroom door open quietly. My mother peeped out, winking and beckoning. She had a tea-pot and a few cups and things on the wash-stand. Meg and Joe were sitting on the bed and the baby, Kevin, was lying there asleep.

'Don't go in! *He's* in there,' mother said in a whisper.

Glumly I remembered. He had been in a temper that morning, shouting curses at mother before he went to work, and slamming the cross-door with a crash. Mother bent to whisper more: 'I left his dinner ready — we'll have ours when he goes out.'

I sat on the bed, dejected, wishing I had gone to Nana's room. Thirsty from chocolate and cigarette-smoke I longed for an orange. Mother got them on Saturday.

'Can I have an orange, mother?'

She made a shut-up gesture. There was a sound in the far room and the door beyond ours opened.

'I'm going out, Missus!'

My mother stood at the door, frowning at us.

'I'm off, Missus,' my father called again. He went down the lobby and the cross-door slammed briefly. So he was all right again — I felt suddenly happy. Mother often said that he went off his head at the full moon.

Back in the lane waiting for the others I watched a fat man starting up his motor-bike. His name was Bill. We always had great gas when he wheeled his bike out of the garage. He'd bounce the starting lever till the engine spluttered *Pop-pop-pop!* When he glided off erectly, goggles and all, we gave him a send-off in verse.

Cecil and Heffernan arrived just in time for the three of us to chant our

57

hymn of hate. Bill was an architect, or a solicitor or something, from the toffy side of Clare Street. For us he was 'Ballacky Bill', but I can't recall and didn't understand then why Bill's face used to turn tomato-red at the vile words we shouted.

When he had pop-pop-popped off we were alone, so we decided to press on with our adventure. Cecil was to do the handing out, Heffernan would take the things from him, and I would keep watch. I don't know how he climbed down into that Aladdin's cave but climb he did, first down, then up again.

'That's mine!' Cecil called. I saw an eagle carved in dark wood coming through the window. Heffernan claimed a marble clock with a cluster of golden angels on it. This was thrust up urgently, followed by Cecil's frightened face. He scrambled out beside us.

'There's a bobby watching!'

We took a cautious peep. The policeman was gazing through the grimy plate glass window in Lincoln Place. He seemed to be staring straight up at us. Scarcely daring to breathe we watched and saw him turn away — he hadn't seen us, after all. We were too unnerved to stay on in the lane.

'Listen,' Cecil said to me when we were near the laneway arch. 'See that? An old hen that don't belong to anybody.'

Right enough there it was, a white hen that was always pecking in the rubbish.

'Why not take her home?' Cecil said. 'You got nothing.'

A great idea! The hen protested, flapping and scratching. Happily I managed to avoid Miss O'Leary and got safely upstairs. There was nobody in, but the old knife was there in its usual place to prise open the cross-door. On our lobby floor the hen looked large, and different from other hens. It darted in under the bench and stared out from the gloom there with quick, sideways jerks of its head. I found a bag of oatmeal. Crouched on my hunkers I kept watching till it strutted out, eagerly pecking.

Not only was the hen a pet, it would lay eggs. My mother would surely be delighted.

A footfall sounded on the stairs! It must be my father coming back, I thought, half pleased imagining his great surprise. It turned out to be Heffernan, carrying the marble clock. At home, he had been told to bring the clock back where he got it, so I could have it if I liked.

It crossed my mind then that Nana was in her room. Taking the clock while Heffernan thundered downstairs I opened the little room door nervously. As usual my granny was at the fire, a shawl about her shoulders, reading her prayer-book. She smiled at me.

'What have you there, Michael?'

'It's a clock I've brought you, Nana.'

My grandmother looked pleased.

'Where have you gotten it from?'

'One of the boys I play with. He's just gone.'

The clock looked lovely on the chest of drawers. I expected more questions, but Nana was charmed with the clock and especially the golden angels.

Having got rid of the clock I went back quietly to my hen and lay beside it. It was marvellous to see, close up, its claws curled in like hands and stepping out, now one, now the other, flat. Thump! Thump! went the yellow beak.

A lot of feet came up the stairs. My mother had arrived with the baby and Meg and Joe, and when she saw the hen she hurried past it into the far room. She was looking cross. 'We couldn't have better luck!' she said. 'Take that unlucky thing out of the house this minute!' There was nothing else for it, so tearfully I brought the hen back to the lane.

My mother knew I had stopped going to school. She didn't mind. She said to Nana: 'He'll be out on the waves of the world soon enough, but don't tell that one Maggie.'

I had grown into a morose, glum-looking boy. 'The black fellow,' a woman called me when a window got broken. 'He's the ring-leader!'

The black fellow. It took me a long time to get over that. What instinctively I longed for — love — was really beyond me to know or understand. I had a vague feeling that I would like very much to get married. It puzzled me that Joe could be so happy, and even with his hair cut short he still had golden curls.

Though we seldom talked or played together now, when we were in bed together and I thought he was asleep I'd sometimes put an arm around him. I could hear him breathing in the darkness and it was comforting to feel the warmth of his body close to mine, yet it brought feelings of guilt. Once when my arm was around his shoulders my brother stirred. I felt shocked and struck against him roughly, pretending to be mumbling in my sleep.

The McCabe girls came to visit Nana and my aunt that summer. It was remarked that they had become quite grown-up girls, and so they had. It was almost unbelievable; here they were, sitting in the same room as myself, in their silky dresses and short skirts. Yet they seemed calm and talked matter-of-factly. Of course one had big tortoiseshell glasses and the other had mousey fair hair. What I covertly admired was the curve of their thighs in their tight-fitting skirts. When they stood up and put on hats and coats and went away the place felt empty.

I was fairly desperate for something I could cherish. I think it was one Saturday afternoon, about then, that I arrived on the top landing breathless, carrying a goat. It had been quite a struggle getting him up all the stairs, but we weren't even allowed into the lobby.

'Well, the cheek of you!' Maggie said at the cross door. 'Take that animal back wherever you got it.'

Neither mother nor Maggie would hear of having a goat in the house. I never felt more mortified. After managing to capture him somewhere along the banks of the Grand Canal, having to bring the goat all the way back again seemed cruel.

I suppose my father, like me, felt the need for company. He put his paper aside one evening after his dinner. Mother was going out. She had her good coat on and the baby in her arms.

'Come on, Mick,' my father said, getting up. 'We'll mosey out and break and monotony. We'll go to the Tivoli or the Queen's.'

I looked at mother anxiously. She winked and nodded.

'Sure yous might as well, Mister.'

Once we had left the house I felt happy to be walking with my father, though it seemed strange. We crossed the tramlines and went into Lincoln Place and around into Westland Row. 'It'll break the monotony, anyway,' my father said, jogging along. We came to a side street where people stood waiting. The theatre door was shut, but over it there hung a solitary light.

The waiting went on, the queue buzzing with snatches of chat. A perfume of oranges floated about, sold by a woman in a shawl. My father bought me one. Pressing near to the queue were a man with a concertina, and another singing, rattling their caps. The people in front began to move — we must be going in!

Stone steps led up. We were all going up so many steps it was hard to believe we'd reached the top. The inside of the theatre was enormous, like Westland Row chapel. 'Come on, Mick,' my father said, and we went down through steps of curved forms to the front row. I sat gaping at the brilliant curtain, like a gigantic sheet of paper with big writing on it.

Music struck up, and a redness like blood lit all the bottom of the curtain. My father took his cap off, bending his grim face with its tight lips as he listened to the music. 'It'll break the monotony,' he said again. I felt thrilled to know that he was listening to the powerful music, and that he was pleased.

On a crash of sound the curtain slid up to reveal another curtain of red plush. This parted in the middle, looped away to either side. Behind it was a scene as bright as day and girls in short skirts dancing. Every one of them smiled up at me. I gaped, amazed. Such music, and beautiful girls, and glittering light — it was a fairyland! 'This is only the chorus, Mick,' he muttered in my ear, a hint of even better things coming. It would all be over soon, I knew then, and felt sad.

A man with a silk hat came on the stage and sang 'Pack up your troubles in your old kit bag and smile — smile — smile!' Leaning across to me my father whispered: 'He's very clever. This is a clever character.' The actor sang another song, the people joined in, everybody clapped. He smiled and bowed, taking his hat off, and his big eyes glittered.

'Hear Hear!' My father shouted, clapping. I felt proud again, as though the singer had been myself.

It was all over too soon, the people were putting on their coats, people were going slowly through the door and down the steps into the ordinary, matter-of-fact street. In the forefront of my miserable disappointment was the thought that school was certain to come back.

Sure enough, one morning an inspector for the school attendance called. He had come before, a Mr Lattimore, but mother said, smartly enough, that I had been sick. 'Well, the Confirmation Classes are starting again,' the inspector said. So there could be no excuse.

The Little Brown
Man

'For the glory of God and the honour of Ireland.' That Monday evening
aunt Maggie was reading out *Our Boys*, the Christian Brothers' comic. It
had a drab appearance but she said it was a lovely book. 'And that is their
motto, the motto of the Brothers,' Maggie said. 'To glorify God and give
honour to Ireland. Oh, a splendid body of men!'

I remembered the morning. I'd felt like a new boy again. Our teacher
was the same ginger-headed Brother but he would scarcely have
remembered me.

The day began with prayers. The Brother stood on his chair to reach a
box high on the wall, in which he turned a key. He opened the little door,
and inside stood a statue of the Blessed Virgin with flowers at her feet.

'Stand up for prayers!' the teacher said. We all stood up, the seats of the
desks forcing us to keep our knees bent. We chanted the prayers together.
On the Brother's table were books, a few pieces of chalk, and the strap.

Next came the Catechism lesson. The teacher read out a question, all the
boys answered together. I went like this:

'Who made the world?'

'GOD MADE THE WORLD!'

'Who is God?'

'GOD IS THE CRATER AN' SUFFERIN' LORD OF HEAVEN AND
EARTH AND OF ALL THINGS!'

'Very good...'

It went on and on, questions we didn't understand, answers we couldn't
pronounce properly. The Brother seemed satisfied to shout the questions
and get in response these explosions of verbiage.

To prepare for Confirmation, the Brother said, we would have a daily
Religious Knowledge half-hour. We must follow the example of our
Suffering Lord because pain had come into the world because of sin. This

was the result of man's fall, the fall of our First Parents, Adam and Eve. That brought pain and sickness and death to the world.

'We must remember that suffering is good for us,' the Brother said. 'Our Lord suffered on the cross, and he offered up his sufferings to God the Father, for us. "Take up your cross and follow me," said Christ. So when you suffer, always remember to offer it up.'

After Religious Knowledge we had all to move up to the front of the class for Catechism Questions. The bishop, when he came to Westland Row church to confirm us, would ask every boy and girl a question. We had to know all the answers.

We were placed in a wide semi-circle near the Brother's table and he went through the Catechism, backwards and forwards, to see how much we knew. He might stop a boy half through his answer and point to the next boy to continue. 'Next!' What Catechism did I know? Frightened, I saw that a number of the boys already had been told to stand aside for failing to give proper answers. 'Next!'

The tall black-skirted man drew nearer. He was pointing to the boy beside me. 'Say the *Confiteor*.' I tried to remember the prayer, feeling lucky because it was one that Nana, a few times, had got me to repeat with her. So when the teacher's finger twitched to me — it did. I had a vision of grey eyes and sandy lashes and the teacher's firm, long face.

'...therefore I beseech the Blessed Mary ever Virgin, Blessed Michael the Archangel, Blessed John the Baptist, the Holy Apostles Peter and Paul and all the Saints to grant me pardon for my sins.'

'Wrong!' the Brother said. 'Try again.'

I knew it was useless. I made the same mistake.

'Stand aside,' he said, pointing to the next boy. Glumly I joined the little waiting group. All had doleful faces and some, shivering, exuded the sour smell of fear. We were like prisoners awaiting execution.

Each of the dunces got six 'biffs'. Hearing the crash, crash, crash and seeing furtively the anguished faces my own turn came nearer, was — now! Lightly he tipped the fingers of my shaking hand to steady it. A blow bit into my palm with incredible force, and stupefied with pain I held my hands out, first the right hand, then the left. We were allowed to stumble back to our desks. The teacher's voice went on matter-of-factly. Squeezed under each arm my swollen hands felt burning hot, beyond endurance. Seemingly it was permitted to nurse the maimed hands briefly before recommencing our studies.

During this respite I glimpsed grey clouds high up in the window. 'When I'm a man I will remember this,' I thought, savagely. 'I'll start something — I'll show up this, I'll put a stop to it!'

The bell rang and I strode out, glancing with deliberate contempt at the Brother's polished boots. 'Bulldog!' the boys called, swinging like monkeys from the railings, running after me. But I was finished with that; I was going home. I told my mother that I'd rather go to any other school. 'Then stay at home till Monday and I'll take you to the National School in Brunswick Street,' she said.

For the remainder of that week I knew the meaning of inward peace, and this inner serenity made all things new.

On Tuesday morning, very early, my mother went shopping and brought me with her. I gloried in the freedom of this day. We went along Nassau Street with all its dainty, different shops, the railings of Trinity College on our right. We came to Clarendon Street, went through the glazed-over South City Market — vegetables, fish, and flowers — and emerged into South Great George's Street.

They were putting out brass name-plates in front of the shops, brass like polished, sun-reflecting gold. Everywhere, it seemed as we walked along, there was a radiance of dazzling light. Pale sunshine gilded pavements the shop-windows reflected, extending the scene, the busy street and sauntering passers-by; all part of a perfect morning.

Not the least part of my happiness was the thought of Saturday, *Wonderland Weekly* day, coming. I have reason to remember that Saturday when I went into McCarthy's shop early, eager but trying to seem calm.

'*Wonderland Weekly*, please,' I said, casually.

'Well... I'll see if it has come in yet.' Miss McCarthy stooped to search under the counter. Holding my breath I saw her straighten up, bearing a bundle of papers tied with cord. She cut the cord, the papers and magazines uncurled as if alive, exuding the perfume of print. 'Here you are, Michael — *Wonderland Weekly*,' she said.

I knew exactly what had happened in the previous instalment of 'The Little Brown Man' — rushing up the stairs two at a time I wondered what had happened since. Of course Maggie was at work, granny dozing in bed, mother nursing her new baby. These were flickering background incidentals. Delight was the tingling emotion I felt at being breathlessly back in the far room, bending over those pages. The coloured pictures, the crispness, the newness of *Wonderland Weekly* evoked a sort of radiance. In the midst of it I realised that I was reading! It was astonishing. I had read half-way down a column of 'The Little Brown Man'! I went back to the beginning to find out how I had done it, whether I could do it again. Yes!

I could have shouted out. My eyes hungrily gobbled the print — I could read!

'Mother! I can read!'

Returning to the pages anxiously I tested my new power. Even big words I could master, slowly, uncertainly, but I could do it. I gasped out the news to Nana. I thought Maggie would never come home.

'Maggie, I've read all "The Little Brown Man"! I can read! I can read!'

A Love Letter

There was no new school for me on Monday. Mother had a sore foot from cutting her toe-nails, she had cut the quick and couldn't walk. I'd read all through my comic and had got another, the *Union Jack*. There was a great detective in it, Sexton Blake and his apprentice, Tinker, and their bloodhound, Pedro. It was a sort of grown-up story but the pictures were great — especially the arch-criminal, Professor Reece, with blazing eyes beneath a domelike forehead.

'You'll get dopey,' my father said, 'reading all them comics.' Intent on reading I hardly noticed what was going on. I knew that Joe was in the nun's school, Meg was five-and-a-half, Kevin three, and little Paudeen had begun to toddle. Miss O'Leary after two years had practically taken over the entire house and was a sort of landlady.

Miss O'Leary, in her shapeless brown cardigan and black straw hat, was forever on the war-path. She would follow customers into the street abusing them. She kept a vengeful eye on everybody in the house, especially the dirt-birds at the top, including Maggie and granny.

Two respectable ladies, dressmakers, who had rooms on the first floor, moved out. Miss O'Leary moved in. The racing tipster, Mr Jack Daw, gave up the second floor. Miss O'Leary took possession, and said she would soon have possession of the top floor as well, rent or no rent.

Soon she had let the second floor, just below us, to a quiet, gentlemanly tenant with a soft grey hat and overcoat and an umbrella. We called him 'Mutt', after the long fellow in the Mutt and Jeff cartoons. He put his name up on one of the doors, J. J. Kennedy, Estate Agent. That was his office and the other room his home. My father was amazingly jealous of Mutt. He'd say: 'That fellow's only a shaper. He never done a hand's turn in his life.'

This morning mother, sitting by the window, interrupted my reading of

66

the *Union Jack*.

'Michael, here's Roseanna on the far side, coming over! What can she want at this hour of a Monday morning — you'd better run down quick, and let her in.'

I dawdled over the comic. Roseanna, anyway, was the granny that was always bringing trouble on us.

'She may have sweets! Can't you hurry — oul O'Leary will be up in arms about the knocking.'

Going down the stairs I heard knocking, and right enough Miss O'Leary's voice raised, barging at Roseanna. The granny was well able for her: 'Will you be good enough, ma'am, to clear out of me bloody road an' let me pass!' And she pushed poor Miss O'Leary to the wall.

'You did perfectly right,' mother said when she heard about it. 'Keep up your dignity, and keep that one at arm's length. She'll burst a blood-vessel some day — and be dead for the rest of her life!'

Roseanna sat down heavily: 'Them stairs will be the death of me yet!' She had brought a parcel, which jingled as she put it on the table.

'If you ask my honest opinion,' Roseanna said, 'that O'Leary one is nothing but a poor old looney. I brung up a few bottles of stout.'

'Sure you're the heart of the roll, Mrs O'Beirne.' Mother was charmed. 'There's cups there on the table — Michael, get the corkscrew!'

Roseanna bent over, closed her knees around the bottle, and the cork went pop. She was wearing a feathered hat, and mother remarked on the hat, and her new coat.

'Sure it's only a rag of a coat I picked up in the sales,' Roseanna said, pulling another cork. 'There y'are, ma'am. And I couldn't put the hat down oncest I seen it. Your health, ma'am.'

'And yours, missus.'

'And how is himself?' Roseanna said, licking her lips.

'Oh the same six-an'-eightpence. With his last shilling down the field, as the saying is, he does be like a devil be times. Which reminds me, I had a terrible dream there, the night before last. I thought I saw Old Nick.'

'Name of the Father, Son and Holy Ghost,' Roseanna said, blessing herself. 'What happened?'

'I'll never forget it,' my mother said. 'He was coming along, getting nearer. Beautifully dressed he was, in a kind of a swallow-tail coat. Silk hat and all. And sez he to me, sez he: "I think you're expecting me, ma'am?"

'"I'm afraid you're making a mistake," sez I quick as lightning — but he kept on coming. And sez he, "No, madam, there is no mistake. I'm quite correct!" Haw haw haw!'

Mother burst out laughing, as usual — she could never be serious for long. 'But it would turn your stomach,' she went on, 'to see the hoofs he had instead of feet. And a tail! I could of died.'

Roseanna looked serious now. She was thinking of why she had come visiting so early.

'I couldn't sit there looking at him in the bed. Poor Paddy. We thought it was only a heavy cold, with all the fishin'. The doctor says it could be the consumption.'

'God sent it isn't that! He was always a steady, sober fella,' my mother said, 'able to keep the pin in his lapel.'

I kept hovering near Roseanna for sweets, but mother said sharply: 'Michael, will you stand from in front of the woman's face!'

'Paddy was always a model. I have an album of snapshots of him,' Roseanna said, 'from the time he was in the Boy Scouts. It's funny, he was always gettin' taken in the little knicks. He looked right well.'

'Sure it's only a cold he has,' mother said warmly. 'He'll get over it, never fear. Are you ready for another drop?'

'I'll pour out me own, ma'am,' Roseanna said. 'Look at the head on that! It'd do your heart good, that an' the smell of it.'

'The Mazie inside can't touch it now,' mother said. 'She's not that well. Just a drop of Wincarnis invalid port and a biscuit.'

The big red-brick building in Brunswick Street, St Andrew's National School, had two different entrances, engraved *Infants' School* and *Boys' School*. I was quite a grown boy, with hardly any schooling though I'd learned how to read.

A boy jingling a bunch of keys let us in. 'Is it Mr O'Neill you want? His room is up there.'

We went up stairs inside, through a crowd of pupils who were tramping down.

'Boys! Halt!'

They all stopped, staring up at the landing above. On the banister-rail was leaning a plump man with glasses.

'Now go down *quietly*. Any more of that whistling and I'll punish every one of you!'

With a fierce expression the teacher went in and closed his door. A moment later my mother knocked on it. 'Come in!'

It was a small, bright room in which Mr O'Neill, the headmaster, sat behind his roll-top desk. He looked fierce with his gleaming pince-nez and his waxed moustache. There was a teacher with him. When the teacher went out my mother said: 'This boy is nine, he's been going to the Christian Brothers but he doesn't seem to like it.'

'Yes?'

'If you could see your way to take him...'

'We're full up.' Mr O'Neill frowned, thinking. His eyes moved behind his glasses and stared at me. 'Very well. Spell pot.'

I felt shocked. Of all the words he could have asked me to spell, this was the worst. I had a vision of home and of Paudeen being held over his potty. It must be Pat he meant, so I spelled out, slowly, 'P, A, T'.

Mr O'Neill banged his hands on the desk.

'God save Ireland!' he said. 'A boy nine years of age, and he can't spell a word of three letters!' He glared at me and inwardly I shrank; he must think me very stupid. Mr O'Neill was disgustedly jabbing his pen in the ink-well, then glaring at mother. 'Give me his name and address!'

Fancy picking on a word like 'pot'! I hated Mr O'Neill, and hated myself for being speechless. Why not tell him that I could have spelled that word? But I only stood gaping. I hadn't even noticed my mother going. Mr O'Neill was too overpowering. He gripped my arm. I glimpsed the frosty edge of his glasses as he hurried me along a windowed corridor of chanting classes.

Mr O'Neill opened a door and beckoned me to follow him. He said a few words to the teacher and went away. The room was sunlit, and I could see through the glass-topped partitions other class-rooms on both sides of this one, the length of the school. I was put sitting among all the other boys, and felt suddenly glad to be here.

The teacher wore a new grey suit. He was over at the blackboard with his face turned sideways, thinking. Smiling to himself he lifted the blackboard and easel away to reveal a map on the wall.

'This is Ireland,' he said. 'What you would see if you were high up in an aeroplane.' He laid a long pointer across the map. 'Galway!' a boy cried. Again he pointed — hands flew up. 'Sir! Sir!' The master nodded to this boy or that, and answers came smartly as he pointed. 'Limerick, Sir!' 'The River Shannon!' 'Belfast!' 'Dublin!'

'Dublin. That's the chief city of Ireland, the capital city.' The teacher looked around the class. 'What boy can tell me why they didn't build it here, right in the middle of Ireland?' That was a puzzle, and we enjoyed having it all explained to us.

From the first day I liked this teacher and the school. A boy named Ronan sat beside me. He had the face of a grown man, which looked unusual on top of his little jersey. In the playground we two kept together.

69

Some of the fellows remembered me as Bulldog. Ronan and I had some deadly tussles with the others, but we usually held our own. After school a pack of children trailed behind me shouting 'Bulldog!'

I knew it was best to ignore the shouts, hoping that eventually they would tire of it and forget. But I would never forget this first day in my new school. And the thing I had learned, which was a cause of so much gladness and relief — the fact that every school is not another Cumberland.

About then was the last time I played around with Cecil Sweeny. Perhaps it was because of what happened that I never wanted to see him again — and what happened was wonderful, and distressing, and very puzzling as well. It had to do with a girl with a red woolly hat.

Cecil, my brother Joe and I had been playing along the quietest part of Merrion Square, opposite the Lawn, and we sat down at the railings. Nearby were several girls, also sitting on the stubby granite wall. I noticed covertly one of them, wearing a red woolly hat, who had long graceful legs, brown curls and a straight nose. She had such a happy laugh, just like my mother's.

Between the girls and me were Cecil and my brother. With pangs of envy I realised that they were chatting to the girls and laughing with them. I wanted desperately to be near the girl with the red hat, instead of sitting miserably by myself.

There were three girls, and three of us. Eventually the five of them who were on friendly terms stood up, and Cecil called to me: 'Come on, we're going to play round at Sewell's!'

First I pretended indifference, then got up and slowly followed them. Sewell's was a horse-dealer's stables in Mount Street beside the Square. I peered in at this beautiful perfumy place with kind of open sections full of hay. The girls and Cecil and Joe were playing with the hay, throwing it at one another.

'Can't you come in?' Cecil shouted. I turned away grimly. Perhaps the girl in the red hat would notice, and even jump up and come over to persuade me. Vain hope! Well at least, I thought glumly as I plodded home, she can't but have noticed how lonely I looked.

Why had I not been able to go in there and make friends with the girl as I wished to? It had been impossible — not just timidity or cowardice. An invisible, powerful hand had gripped and held me.

At home I felt more lonely than ever. When I thought of them happily playing in the hay my misery increased so much that I felt desperate. Then came a daring idea. I felt overjoyed at the thought of it.

Feeling sure that anyone who saw me must have guessed my purpose, I stealthily brought pen and paper into the far room, and sat down at a little table in a corner. By crouching over the paper — a page torn from my copy-book — I hoped to hide what I was doing; I uncorked the ink-bottle, dipped in the pen...

At this last moment — only then — the truth dawned on me. Oh stupid, stupid, stupid! I drew a deep breath of disgust. How could I write to the girl when I knew neither her name nor her address?

The sinking fear that I was 'wanting' reminded me of long ago, the time aunt Crissy had said, 'Ain't we very stupid.' I still felt badly about that — felt furious resentment. Strangely, the change of mood made life less dark. Some day, I thought, I'd prove that I was far from stupid: clever in fact, just as clever as anybody else!

What Makes Big
People Grumpy?

Sunday trams clattered past on the Nelson Pillar-Kingstown-Dalkey line as
Maggie and I walked on, and on, through dusty summer heat to Herbert
Park. It was far, near Ballsbridge, yet not far enough to take the tram. We
always walked.

At last came the corner where we would turn into the tree-lined road of
Herbert Park. It was a clean, smooth, special kind of footpath. Here and
there the sunlit, pale grey surface glittered, as though arrows of light
leaped up. Maggie said it must be sand from the seashore mixed with the
cement, and the sandy bits gleamed.

This novelty banished my tiredness as we walked on, watching for the
diamond flashes. In the park we sauntered by the pond where ducks
floated, or turned tail-up feeding. A grown man was kneeling by his
handsome toy yacht, adjusting the rigging. It showed how strong a breeze
was blowing, for the sails flip-fluttered; then away the yacht sped, turning
over, almost, but righting itself to sail on. The man went loping around to
meet it at the opposite side after its voyage. One day, I thought doubtfully,
I might own a yacht like that.

One thing I knew for certain, as we made our way around the pond: the
next time we came, I'd bring a jampot. Because by standing at the edge,
gazing down, I saw in the clear depths dozens of pinkeens, darting as one
in and out, where an underground pipe ended as a weed-furred circle. It
would be a glass jampot with a cord handle, and walking along I'd glance
down at the narrow dark backs or pause to examine my pinkeens, alive and
swimming, staring at me round-eyed through the glass.

It was fairly boring just strolling around like all the other Sunday
strollers. We looked at the flower-beds. There were roses, pansies, red-hot
pokers, every kind, and Maggie remarked on the perfume they gave and
how beautiful they looked.

She said then that we might as well stroll over to the summerhouse and sit down for a while. The summerhouse was a lonely dark hut near which the river Dodder flowed. It was an isolated spot, and somehow saddening.

'Oh, feel that,' Maggie said stooping. 'The grass is bone dry. We could sit down here and watch the river.'

She said if we stayed very quiet we might see a kingfisher streak past, or a trout might leap out of the water. There was nothing to be heard except the flowing river's whisper, or once or twice, close to your ear, an insect's tiny trump. Maggie reached out her hand and plucked a buttercup, and held it near her chin.

'We used to make daisy-chains,' she said, 'when I was a little girl.'

She held the buttercup against my chin.

'What's that for, Maggie?'

'To see if you're jealous,' she said, laughing.

'Am I jealous?'

Still holding the buttercup under my chin she said your skin reflects it — either yellow or green. If it showed green you were jealous, if yellow, not. She looked closely to see.

'Oh, well. I'd say you could be jealous, very jealous,' Maggie said, amused, and threw the buttercup away. From a distant clock-tower, silvering the silence, chimes came 'Ding, dong; dong ding dong!' It was a far-away sound, delicate, wistful, fading away.

'There goes five,' Maggie said. 'How the time flies!'

We stood up and made sure we had forgotten nothing, and prepared to go home. By starting now, we would be home by tea-time, Maggie said. Then she gave a little sigh. 'It's a pity, such a beautiful Sunday evening, but all good things come to an end.'

'I'm bringing a jampot next Sunday,' I told her, 'for pinkeens.'

After Sunday Monday comes, and settling into the new school made life different, and earnest. Confirmation was only a few weeks away, but not for us — it would be for the bigger boys, in Beaver's class. Beaver had a jet-black beard and a terrible temper, and when he got his rag out he'd fire the strap at a fellow, right across the room.

Our turn for Confirmation would come next year. Meanwhile our class had suddenly moved up to Second and we all had to get new books. We thought we might be getting a new teacher too, maybe Mr Flanagan or his smaller brother, Mr Flanagan, but no. Luckily our own teacher, Mr McManus, moved up with us.

Every morning we started with prayers. All the glass partitions were folded away and you could see the other classes, and they all could see

Mr O'Neill standing up on a table to say his prayers, and we with him. Then the lessons began.

Right away we had our Catechisms open on our desks. That was the Religious Lesson. We chanted the questions and answers like a song. Mr McManus walked up and down between the desks. Sometimes he had a strap with him, and if a fellow deserved it for horseplay he'd get a biff or two. I hardly ever got slapped now.

As well as religion we had sums, geography and reading. Then came a surprise — a completely new sort of lesson. The teacher began to explain. We were about to learn a language. There were about three dialects in it, he said, but he would teach us the Munster dialect. 'I suppose the best way to learn a language... Well, first we need to know the names of things. For example...'

He picked up the square wooden chalk-box, pointed at it, and said: 'Buska!' With gusto we all repeated: 'Buska!' And a piece of chalk: 'Piecea calk.'

It was a marvellous, exciting lesson. It turned out that this was our own proper language because we were Irish, and this language was the Irish way of saying things. It was funny calling the blackboard 'More dove', and trying to think of a cow and ass as 'Mo agus Assil'. Speedily we picked up phrases, and there was no lack of volunteers when Mr McManus asked us to 'Oscal an dhoriz' — half a dozen or more rushed to open the door, but Mr McManus called 'Halt!'

'We must remember our manners,' he said. 'I should have said: "Oscal an dhoriz, mash eye though helly" — "If you please."'

How amazing it was to discover that we had been speaking English, a foreign tongue, and that this queer new language we were learning was Irish, our own! It was a real shock; we had been talking like foreigners and never knew... no wonder the Sinn Feiners were fighting the Black and Tans.

I wondered if Maggie knew this. It would be something surprising to tell mother and Maggie. This Irish, this 'Neel' for No and 'Thaw' for Yes, was the way we should be talking all the time!

The trouble was, when you heard an Irish word you'd be reminded of an English word that hadn't the same meaning at all. Often the result was funny. When the novelty wore off, all that was left was a language hard to learn. Was it because I was stupid? Just after learning how to read I was back where I started; the different-looking print, the different words left me puzzled all over again.

It was a bright and happy school, just the same. Even when we were doing sums in Irish you wouldn't be punished for being stupid. I felt sure I must be stupid in many ways, and that was a sad thing; but I knew that in some one way I'd make up for it, some day — and shine.

Not all the Irish was as hard as Irish sums. There was a story in our Irish book, *Leabhar na Gaelige*, from which in a glowing haze of memory there still leaps — a white fairy horse. The words are with me yet, about 'Phoul a Phouca ar na smeara dubha' — the white Fairy Horse that jumps over the blackberry bushes in October.

When Mr McManus explained this to us in English, hands in his trouser pockets as he sat against his table, it was splendid. He told us what a poetic way the Irish have, describing ordinary happenings to show that they are magical — like when in winter the blackberries are blighted by the frost. Only, for the Irish poet, the frost comes to life as a white fairy horse.

Although school was all right, it was still school, where you had to go day after day. The master could do what he liked, but we boys had to do what we were told.

It was different for big people: they could go to work. It must be a great feeling, I thought, to be able to go to work and to have so much freedom. What I wondered about a great deal was that big people so often seemed cross and inclined to be fighting. Why was that?

At home these evenings I'd always be bent over a comic and when the comic was read I'd be mooching around, up to some mischief or other. One evening while granny dozed I went to the chest of drawers and rummaged among Maggie's things.

Maggie herself often rummaged in one of the top drawers, full of old papers and letters and photographs. She might sometimes get into a sad mood doing this and just stand staring at nothing. I remembered seeing a roundy glass thing with moving lights in it which Maggie kept in the small box. I tried to find it but she had the box locked. I had to be content with looking at a silver spider, a brooch with eyes and all and with his legs splayed out, but Maggie came in that very minute and gave me a crack across the ear.

'Get away from there!' she said viciously. She had a square, glum face on her and she looked smaller in her long black weekday coat. 'I'm only raging,' she said to granny. 'I'll be getting the sack yet. That Helena Moloney one is watching me, and shish she to me today, shish she: "Did you not get that done yet?"'

'You're a terrible worrier,' granny said. 'She didn't mean —'

'She did mean!' Maggie snapped. 'It was a cut, because I'm too slow, that's what! Them young ones beside me, only in it a few weeks, are able to do twice as much. They're like lightning — then they'd be sitting idle. One of two of them give me a hand, decent enough, otherwise I don't know what I'd do.'

Granny had the table set and Maggie made the tea. Though she still talked about work, my aunt had got into good humour again because she was thinking about Mr Heezler, the works manager.

'There's no doubt about it,' Maggie said, 'Mr Heezler is a gentleman to his finger-tips. Always perfectly correct, no matter what happens. They made some mistake in the printing department today, and the foreman printer brought it up to Mr Heezler. Do you think he got flustered? Not a bit. I call tell you the foreman was red in the face, though, with his long slip of paper in his hand.

'Mr Heezler simply pointed to his desk for the foreman to lay down the paper. Well, Mr Heezler took one look at the paper, picked it up between finger and thumb, and said to the foreman: "Query that." Nothing else. Just: "Query that", in a kind of scornful tone of voice. That's breeding — is there any of the jam left?'

There was no jam left, and granny had forgotten to buy more.

'I told you to get a pot of mixed jam today in Findlater's,' Maggie said. 'But there's no use talking to you. You won't forget your quarter-ounce of snuff, I'll wager!'

'Your tongue is always going like the clappers of a bellows,' granny said. 'I'll get the jam tomorrow.'

'Oh the old story — locking the stable door when the horse has bolted!'

'I wish to God I was miles away,' granny said. 'I'm not too well at all. And between the rows in there, and that madwoman below, and now you —'

'Maybe you'd better get yourself away to Dalkey for a week,' Maggie said. 'The change of air will do you good.'

My aunt Maggie O'Reilly.

Aunt Maggie's
Romance

When Maggie brought Nana in the train to Dalkey she'd have loved to stay there herself — the sun was splitting the trees. She had to be back at her work, like I had to be at school. So it was great when Saturday came round again.

I used to sit on the top flight of stairs beside the big back window. With its view of the National Picture Gallery and the green Duke's Lawn this window was a picture in itself, especially when everything was sunlit. But this day everything was grey, the cloudy sky, the shiny roofs of backyard sheds. Sometimes the invisible air took shape as grey wraiths dancing through the rain, which tinkled like a dulcimer down in some puddle. Our window rattled, and the wet glass made the National Gallery look tattered.

In happy isolation I was chanting softly, 'Rain, rain, go away, come another sunny day,' hugging my knees and gazing at the downpour. I never thought about my aunt being out in it until she came home drenched. She did her shopping on Saturday, the half day, and she was after walking all the way from Sackville Street — the trams were packed. Of course Maggie, embracing her rain-sodden parcels, was only fit to be tied.

There was no 'Hello' or 'How are you?' from the squelching figure grimly making her way up the last flight. She only growled: 'Move yourself there, you — can't you see I'm drippin'.' Passing me she added, crossly: 'Did the Society man come yet?'

Mother often said that Maggie was a real old maid. She fussed over paying her way without fail for every little thing. She even had money saved up in the Post Office, mother said.

Maggie's post-office account went back to the time she began working. That was in John Faulkiner's when she was a girl — the firm was still there in Sackville Street. Those had been happy days for Maggie. She often said about the foreman printer, Tony, being her beau and he would cut his right hand off for her. I wondered what a dress dance might be. They went to that one time, and my aunt wore a truly magnificent cloak with a matching button. But that had been long, long ago and Tony had got married since.

Distantly, down below, the hall-door banged. Somebody was coming up. Around the banisters appeared a glistening yellow oilskin and I knew it was the new Society man, who came now that our Mr Noonan was sick. He came gazing up at me, water dripping from his cape, his red face one glad smile.

It was nice to see Mr Hennessy because it broke the monotony. Also this new Society man had a special trick he could do. It was wonderful to see the way his teeth enlarged under his wide sandy moustache. While he stood waiting on the landing, staring down at me, he could waggle his teeth.

'Hello there!' he boomed, plodding up. 'Is Miss O'Reilly in?'

I told him yes, I'd get her. She wasn't speaking to mother because of something that was missing from the top drawer — aunt Maggie said for two pins she would pack up everything and run mad out of it. The way she had run mad out at lunch-time, I supposed, to hurry back to Faulkiner's, where Tony had put a screen around her to keep off the draughts.

Now I hovered at her door. 'Maggie, it's the Society man.'

'Coming, Mr Hennessy, coming!' she called over my head. 'I'll be with you in just a minute.'

I snatched the chance to sidle in while she was foostering at the chest of drawers. The little box inlaid with mother-o'-pearl was in the top left-hand drawer — the one full of sovereigns that granny got when she was married. There was always a solemn smell when Maggie opened this top drawer. It was a musky kind of smell. The album was kept there in a softness of ribbons and silk, and an oval-shaped bottle of eau-de-Cologne.

What I watched for was when she'd put the key in the box, open the lid, and take out a satin-lined tray to get the Society book. Under the grey book lay a bundle of old letters, and somewhere beneath these, I knew, must be the button with its moving lights.

While my aunt searched for her key the Society man outside gave an impatient cough. Maggie was flustered. I heard her whisper fiercely, to herself: 'Sweet Lord! Was there ever such a den of thieves!'

She grabbed up her key, got the book and hurried out, leaving the door slightly ajar. From outside could be heard all this how-are-you, big people's talk.

79

'That's a day and a half, Miss O'Reilly.'

'Don't be talking! I'm only in myself, all the way from Moore Street on Shanks' mare. It's more like a cloudburst.'

'The world is coming to an end. They say it's all the heavy artillery brings on the rain.'

'Sure we'll all be web-footed,' Maggie said, laughing. 'There's no going out these days unless you go in somewhere, like the pictures.'

'You're fond of the pictures, Miss? Did you see Charlie Chaplin? I nearly died laughing, I could see it again.'

I was right beside the chest of drawers. Leaning against it I slid a finger along the bevelled edge of the top one, where the little box was. The button was in there. It would be easy enough to get it, just to look at it. Only Maggie would be sure to come in! I pressed my back against the drawers, watching the almost-shut door. They were laughing, it was too good a chance to miss.

Shockingly the door moved, but she had only closed it. I slewed around, gazing at the picture above the chest of drawers. A picture of the sea, with a pale, glossy wave about to crash on the shore — rising up, curling over foam-crested, frozen. Half-accidentally I'd pulled the drawer wide open. The Society man's laugh rattled like the window as with fluttering heart I gripped the box. She had left the key — here was the fancy button in my hand!

Across my palm it cast an amber glow. Countless gold specks were glistening within the shining dome. My hand shook, and all the starry lights inside the button quivered. 'No, indeed I won't.'

The door was opening. I stared at it horrified, too frighted to move.

'Indeed I won't — and thank *you*, Mr Hennessy.'

'For nothing. Well cheery-pip, ducky. I'll be off, I think it's clearing.'

'Tomorrow, then — and mind yourself on them stairs.'

'Goodbye now.'

'Goodbye, Mr Hennessy.'

She was back in the room, saw the open drawer and me beside it. She towered high above me, raging. A hand slapped down, I dropped the button, wriggled past her and was gone.

Even though it was Sunday the next day my aunt was in the best of humour. She even spoke to my mother, and remarked that she would go out early after dinner — it had turned out such a lovely day.

'I'll come with you, Maggie,' I said.

'You, is it?' She had a face on her. 'After yesterday?' She muttered then, by the way to herself: 'That fellow is getting as bold as brass.'

I felt sure she was only pretending to be 'out' with me. She only needed to be coaxed: 'Aw, auntie Maggie! Don't you always take me with you — aw, go on!'

'Shut up — or else get out!'

It wasn't that she was raging, she hardly noticed me at all really. She bustled about as if I wasn't there. It was amazing the care she took washing her face and her hands, even cleaning her nails, finger and toe! She washed her feet in the small tin basin.

As soon as dinner was over my aunt began to fuss around again, getting ready to go out. From the long middle drawer she carefully lifted her new fawn coat. She went over and over to the mirror nailed up beside the window. 'Ain't it pretty?' she said, half to herself, fixing and re-fixing her blue straw hat. The fawn coat hung on her in its own perfect folds, down to her buttoned-up boots. I had never seen my aunt looking so nice.

'Away! away!' She flicked me off impatiently, opening the top left-hand drawer. She tipped her ears with the glass cork of eau-de-Cologne, then examined her handbag. 'Don't ever let me see you at this drawer again,' she said, 'or next or near it. Remember now. Them things are not to be touched!'

Maggie put on a gold ring, curving her fingers back to admire the little diamond in it. The ring made a bulge when she drew on her lavender glove.

'Is it going to be fine?'

We both gazed out at the blue sky.

'Sure it's a beautiful day,' she said, good-humouredly. 'No need to take the gamp.' She made a concentrated frown, and shook a finger at me. 'Don't you forget! Next or near them things you're not to go!'

The door closed after her. The hall-door slammed.

It was a mournful thing to be alone and to know that she didn't care, and didn't want me. I thought of going round to the Museum, but that was an awful old place any day, let alone on a Sunday. Mooching down the stairs I thought how dull everything was, even our big back window showed a dreary view.

There was no sign of life. There was nowhere to go. There was nothing around but the Museum, the old Lawn and the Picture Gallery. You needed someone big to take you further — and you'd still be in Sunday, even then.

I stood poised in surprise at the hall-door, then quickly came in again and closed it. Over there at the Mont Clare corner my aunt was waiting. I knew instantly that she was waiting for him: that man with the waggley teeth. I remembered the way they'd been talking.

There came over me a sickening feeling, a feeling of loss and of shame. It weighed me down as I wearily climbed the stairs. I went into Maggie's room and sat on the edge of a chair, baffled. Could it really be true? I went into the far room because from there you could see, and sure enough there she was down below, still waiting!

As I watched she began to stroll sedately back and forth, a dumpy figure even in her new fawn coat. I wanted to shout out to mother and Meg to come and look. Uneasily I thought that this was a kind of a secret between my aunt Maggie and me — and anyway, something that shouldn't be mentioned.

All of a sudden my mother said: 'Michael! What are you up to at that window?'

'It's Maggie.' With a gasp of relief I made the revelation. 'She's across there waiting for the Society man.'

'She is not,' Meg said. My sister was only seven, but in ways she was much quicker than me. They couldn't believe it. They jumped up and rushed to the window just the same. Their faces were sideways to the glass, one high and one low, watching.

'It's no joke,' mother said. 'There she is.'

Meg gave a little-girl giggle. 'Will you look at the waddle of her!'

'Well I... Throwing her hat at Hennessy — that oul gather-'em-up,' mother said in disgust. 'With his bike and his blarney!'

They kept staring at the corner opposite.

'It's as good as the Palace picture house,' Meg said.

'Well after *that*!' my mother said, meaning there were no more wonders left. 'The clever kinat!'

'But maybe he wants to be her friend,' my sister said. 'You have to wait and see, as Mr Asquith says.'

'What do you know about Mr Asquith,' mother said absently, intent on the distant Maggie in her Sunday best.

They seemed rooted to the spot; and just gazed and gazed. With two of them there I couldn't see a thing — only the blank, deserted pavement opposite. Then I had an inspiration. Why not slip into Maggie's room while the coast was clear, open the box and —

'Here she is coming back.'

'Not she! There you are,' my mother said, 'it's only walking up and down she is. I wouldn't be surprised if he was after giving her the long drop.'

'She'll be raging,' Meg said.

As I edged over to the door, mother said: 'There's no sign of her now, she must have went. Her face was flaming!'

Within seconds I was back in Maggie's room. Especially just now, while Nana was away, the neatness of the little room was a reproof. Stiff lace curtains were reflected in the polished lino, there were two chairs with leather seats, on the drawers the silent clock with golden angels under a painted wave.

I held my breath, listening, and pulled the top drawer open but the little box was locked. Yes — the key was underneath. I felt it sink into place and softly turn, and the satin-lined, faded interior lay open. Once more the button was in my hand, glowing with its own strange life. I brooded over it. On the polished mahogany when I held it tilted forward two golden buttons beamed.

The door. Very quietly, almost stealthily it opened and my aunt came in. She closed the door gently and turning, saw me with surprise.

'Oh, it's you,' she said, putting her gloves down on the button. She went on quite politely, like a visitor: 'I didn't go too far. Didn't feel like it, somehow. And it looked like rain.'

I gazed out at the rooftops. The sky was blue. Maggie stood taking hat-pins out of her blue hat. Then she stared.

'Dear, oh, dear, you've been at the drawer again,' she said, and taking up her gloves she saw the button. I felt myself shivering.

'Run off with you now,' my aunt said, mildly. She picked up the button and held it lightly on her palm, gazing at it. 'There now,' she coaxed, 'be a good little boy. Go and play in the Lawn, it's a fine sunny evening.'

Why had she not gone to Dalkey, I wondered, to see granny? There was a row of some sort going on there. I wasn't supposed to know, but I was to be in Dalkey the following Sunday with Maggie, and when that time came something of what was going on would dawn on me.

Music, Tears
and
Laughter

All this time I knew that a sort of war was going on in Ireland. In Dublin hand grenades were thrown, shots fired, houses searched. Lorries full of British soldiers, with wire netting to protect them — 'like monkeys in a cage', one of our street jibes went — tore along the streets and it was dangerous to be out late. After half nine at night you'd hear nothing but the occasional roar-past of an army lorry.

The Black and Tans were the worst, Maggie said, and we were never to play at running games around the Lawn. All they wanted was an excuse to open fire. My nerves used to tighten at sight of a lorry-load of Black and Tans, and I made sure to be walking real slow.

It was near the Duke's Lawn that I met my great friend David Hassett. He was my own age, nine-and-a-half. His father was in the Civil Service, wearing a uniform with one sleeve empty, and a peaked cap. He had been wounded in the war. David Hassett and his parents and an older sister lived in the basement of a house in Merrion Square.

David was a neat and very perfect boy. I was lucky to have met him. He had black straight hair and dark brown eyes with a direct, calm gaze. He was always nicely dressed in a navy-blue suit — even Miss O'Leary was polite to him when he knocked at our hall-door. David and I became real chums.

There used to be two Italian men, musicians, whom we often stood to watch and listen to. One played a barrel-organ, called a hurdy-gurdy, which had only one leg. On top of this, or on his shoulder as he turned the handle playing, would sit a watchful monkey with a pink fez on his head. This little fellow had a most intelligent expression. Whereas his master seemed careless, with a cheeky grin, the dressed-up monkey had a worried, sharp-eyed little face. You'd think he was counting the takings, and while the organ-grinder played on cheerfully his pet would jump down to pick up pennies and hold out his little hat for more, in urgent appeal.

The other Italian man, a harpist, had a solemn, listening posture. He totally ignored the public. With head bent reverently he listened to himself playing the harp. In the quiet of the evening, in the calm sedateness of Merrion Square, the notes of the harp-strings were beautiful and sad.

We took it for granted that the man was Irish, since he played a harp. This instrument was enormous, with a beautiful curvy top from which hung its velvet green cloak. The harpist's thumbs curled back, his fingers plucking. Even more impressive than the lovely harp shape was the way the strings, almost invisible, rose up across it. One day he got annoyed and shouted: 'You-all go away to Heel!' Then we knew he was a foreigner.

The week that was bringing me nearer to next Sunday, and to Dalkey, went by with surprising quickness. For that entire week I had abandoned my dislike of carpentry, and had given myself over to woodwork. The great harp, now part of the Georgian street scene of Dublin, held me in its magic thrall. I wanted to own, and play, a harp like that. There was nothing for it — my need was so urgent — but to make one.

Sitting on the sofa in the far room I'd noticed a broken part from which the stuffing protruded. It was a real horse-hair sofa. Carefully pulling one of the hairs, I found that it came out fairly willingly and was incredibly long. Also it had an elastic toughness, a hair from a horse's tail. A dozen or so of these and my harp was half-made.

The difficult part was the wretched woodwork. I wondered how to change a piece of thick, straight wood into a lovely curvy top, impressive enough for my harp. With one of his oval carpenter's pencils I marked out the shape, and with a bread-knife pared and pared the timber until the shape stood out. I could have shouted for joy. I lovingly smoothed it with sandpaper, gloating over my harp coming to life — the curving top, the strings!

What was still to be done, a V-style pair of uprights on a wooden base, quickly came into position firmly nailed to the top. Saturday came, a morning of crouched-over, breathless, tense excitement, with my brother Joe watchfully handing me nails. I hammered in two rows of these to hold the horse-hair strings.

An hour later my home-made harp was ready. Here and there a nail had cracked the frame and the harp was inclined to lean sideways, but no matter — I was ready to play. There was a faint plonk, plonk. Joe bent his ear closer to listen, a string broke, and in the fight that followed the whole harp fell asunder.

With the sharp eyes of defeat I saw my puny, ridiculous attempt for what it was. Like my other attempts to make something — my Zeppelin, a gas-filled sausage balloon that wouldn't fly, my yacht with handkerchiefs for sails that wouldn't even float!

My entire life was a failure I decided miserably, and all because I was a 'stupo', as mother might have said. Trying to find consolation I thought, as I had often done before, about my mother's people. All of them — or anyway the ones we knew about — were most superior.

There was Jim Roe, for example, actually the Superior of a Christian Brothers' College in India, dressed all in white. His photo was there in Maggie's album, standing on the college lawn backed by two hundred scholars and the big white building. Then there was Tom Coombes, a cousin high up in the British Army in Africa. It was hard to make him out lined up with troops all wearing ostrich-feather hats, standing to attention being inspected by King Edward under the enormous trees.

As well, there was the Little Woman who was granny's sister — Mrs Howard. She had married a British Army Commander or something, she being such a magnificent cook. He said she must come with him every-where the army went, and they sailed into Darkest Africa along the River Niger. In spite of it all the Little Woman sometimes came to visit us!

One time, when she happened to drop in, being in town, it seemed like a happy coincidence that we had a tropical fish in the house. It was my goldfish in a round glass globe, placed on the chest of drawers. Maggie said it was all right for me to keep it there as it was a regular ornament, and tropical.

The goldfish opened its mouth wide and a crumb of ant's egg went rocking slowly upward. Flicking its tail, gliding smoothly around its bowl, the fish stared out with its flat circular eyes.

Mrs Howard, of course, was delighted. Delighted to see her sister Nana, delighted to see the goldfish. The Little Woman had a tropical, wrinkled face and black protruding eyes. She had the amazed expression of a small pom dog. She had peacock feathers on her hat and rings on all her fingers. She was flighty, Maggie said.

'A goldfish, I declare!' she said in quick, decisive tones. 'This is Michael's pet, I'll wager! It *is* Michael, isn't it — I'd scarcely know you. Go tell your mother Mrs Howard is here.'

Closing the door on my way out I heard the visitor laughing. She had a pealing laugh and was so jolly and commending you'd know she was some-body special.

When mother came in the two of them met in an uproar of greetings and laughter. 'It's younger you're getting, Teazie!' Mrs Howard cried, giving granny an astonished nod to confirm it. 'Ah, here's a woman after my own heart!' she declared, her hands, laden with gold and black rings, lying palms up on her lap.

The moment my mother heard Mrs Howard was there she had gone to the mirror to tidy her hair and lick a red pill-box to colour her cheeks.

'Though I and Bessie are not *speaking*,' Mrs Howard was saying when I went back to the room. 'I wouldn't *bother* if Joe was a young man. But to think of marrying again at his age — he must be nearly seventy! It's giving the place away.'

She picked up her glass of stout. Nana, sitting beshawled in her armchair, inquired: 'And you mean to tell me Bessie still has both the cottages?'

'She *claims* to have. I *certainly* refuse to give up mine — where else have I to go? Of course Bessie imagines she can wind Joe round her little finger.'

Sipping her small glass of Wincarnis, Nana eyed Mrs Howard serenely.

'Who is it he's thinking of taking?'

'Oh the man's a fool,' Mrs Howard said contemptuously. 'A perfect fool — though he is my own brother.'

The door opened.

'Why, Teazie!' Mrs Howard had immediately swung round, glaring up at my mother. 'Come in, come in, give us a laugh — I've been dying for a good laugh for weeks! Haw haw haw!' When she threw her head back, laughing, all her gold teeth glimmered.

'Haw haw haw!' mother chortled. 'Here's a sight for sore eyes!'

'It's younger you're getting, Teazie...'

The Coolness in
Dalkey

Immediately after Mass on Sunday, Maggie said, she would bring me to Dalkey to see granny. When she came back from Mass she was going around with her good hat on, distracted, flying here and there or stooping with the long steel button-hook to check that her patent-leather boots were fully buttoned. As I came to the cross door I saw her shiny boots and her face pink with excitement. She turned from the wash-basin out on the landing, towel on arm.

'Sweet Lord! Are you not ready *yet*?'

'Yes I am!'

Her face took on her square, mournful expression.

'Is that what you call ready! Look at that collar — just look! Go and get a clean collar this minute, and polish them boots.'

'This is my best collar, Maggie. I'll turn it inside out.'

'Sweet Lord be my salvation! Such a crew!' She hurried past me with the towel and hung it up. 'Don't think for one moment you're coming with *me* in that condition.'

Maggie's unexpected tantrums overshadowed life at times, like passing rainclouds. They were much more frequent than the occasional row in the Far Room — which depressed all concerned, like an overcast, black day. Well these things couldn't be helped. Anyway, Maggie saw to it that when I went with her I was always neat and clean.

When we arrived in Dalkey we called first of all, as before, to the Little Woman to see Nana. The hallway of this house was cramped and shadowy, but the room where granny sat looked bright. She was making wonderful strides, the Little Woman said, simply wonderful strides.

'It's the Dalkey air,' she told Maggie. 'The sea air is as good as a tonic. There's nothing like it — and of course the complete change works wonders.'

I stood in the parlour gaping at them, listening open-mouthed.

'Run along to Miss Archbold, Michael!' Mrs Howard said sharply. 'You can come back for tea in an hour. Be sure to tell Miss Archbold that *I* said you are to have tea here, with *us*.'

Miss Archbold — that was Bessie, of course. I wasn't used to thinking of her as Miss Archbold. I went reluctantly into the silent, sunlit lane, and hesitantly down the long tiled hall to Bessie's kitchen. The air held a delightful spicy smell, like cloves. By the range stood the upright little figure with a face like Nana's — only Nana never looked so cross.

'Michael, is it? And to what do we owe the pleasure of this visit?' asked the mournful voice. She added more alertly: 'Is Maggie with you?'

'She's with Nana.'

'Oh! In Howard's, I suppose?'

'Yes, aunt Bessie. I'm to go back for my tea later on. Mrs Howard said to say that she said so.'

Aunt Bessie stooped and poked at the range fire. She seemed to be muttering to herself. She gave me a stare.

'No doubt you'd like to see the hens, child — off you pop into the yard.'

I heard a rattle like torn paper. It came from the breeding-cage.

'Aunt Bessie, do those canaries belong to uncle Joe?'

'They certainly do!'

I was afraid to say more. The door into the yard wailed as I pushed it open and stood in front of the run. The hens made a mad dash to the wire netting. There wasn't even a bit of grass to give them, so they got nothing.

It was like a little grey box, with nothing but hungry hens to look at. I thought of my friend David Hassett, and how I could have been playing with him. After brooding for ages I decided to go back. The door wailed again, and this time uncle Joe was in the kitchen.

Uncle Joe was a man of about sixty with a long nose curving over his grey moustache. The sleeves of his thick blue suit were shortened from the way he had sat down, joining his hands between his knees. Both his hairy wrists had blue tattoo marks.

'Well, he certainly did not!' Bessie was saying in her sensible, worldly tones. 'And he'd turn in his grave if he could hear you saying such a thing. Matthew left them cottages to the two girls. The two girls, them were his very words.'

'But Mr Ledwidge says—'

'Now that's enough!'

Joe leaned forward, one hand out, appealing.

'I'm only saying these cottages belongs to me by law; I have papers to prove it. I don't want any trouble over this, and there's no need for it. What do the two of yous want with two cottages?'

Bessie stood like an iron poker. 'What on earth do you mean?'

In the dusk Joe's face looked black above his hard white collar.

'You know very well what I mean, Bessie. You wouldn't be going far, only across the road. Yous 'ud be company for each other —'

'You're right, I wouldn't be going far. I wouldn't be going a-tall a-tall — the cheek of you! This is my home, and who has a better right to it? That bony-faced Hanny I suppose — as if one wasn't enough for you!'

'I'm only saying!'

'Say no more!' Cutting him short, sharp as a breadknife, Bessie clicked her tongue with rage and the canaries warbled She was bending to the open oven door with a cloth over her hands. Out came a pie, filling the room with a delicious perfume.

'Did you see who's here?' Joe said in a guarded manner. I had been standing at the door, afraid to come in on the conversation.

'Oh that's Michael,' she said indifferently. 'It seems Maggie is across in Howard's — and this was sent here on a visit, if you please.' She gave a little nod at me. 'Well then, you've seen the hens?'

'Yes.'

It was uncomfortably silent till Joe spoke: 'How is your granny keeping?'

'Very well, thank you.'

'Wouldn't it surprise you,' Bessie said. 'When you think of the young Roes, and Goo Byrne's pair — lively as linnets. With this you have to push to get a move at all.'

Sullenly I looked at her and looked away. I was numb with dismay and hidden rage. I knew they were talking about me — did Bessie think I was too stupid to know? I felt a dull anger against some vague feeling of injustice. Then a step sounded in the hall. I saw the familiar, square shape of my aunt Maggie coming.

'The prodigal returns,' Bessie said in her mournful, more friendly voice. My aunt was looking pleased. She was telling Bessie how much better Nana was, quite well enough to come home this evening. 'I'll bring her over to see you before we go.'

Bessie nodded with pretended indifference. 'And how's Teazie?'

'Do you need to ask? Teazie is herself. "When you see Bessie," shish she, "tell her I'll get out to Dalkey before the summer's over," shish she. Although I don't see how...'

'Ach, hasn't she been saying that for years. Can't you sit down? I never

90

did know such an oddity as you are.'

Laughing, Maggie got a chair. It was amazing how much at home, and at ease, she was here.

'You haven't a word for me at all,' Joe said, as she sat down. 'How are you, Maggie?'

Maggie looked startled, then she tittered.

'It must be the sun in my eyes, I didn't see a bit of you. H'm. I'm very well, thank God.' A chill had crept into her voice. 'There's so many rumours going the rounds, to tell the truth I didn't think I'd see you here at all.'

'Oh, rumours.' After a moment Joe said, turning an examining gaze on me, 'Michael's growing to be quite a young man now.'

'Yes, isn't he getting tall — bigger than myself now,' Maggie said, laughing. 'He'll be ten in April.'

I stood up, self-conscious as well as resentful.

'Mrs Howard said I'm to go back in an hour.'

'Very well,' Bessie said. 'By all means go back to Mrs Howard.'

'Though I'm sure he'd like a slice of that nice pie I see,' Maggie said good-humouredly.

Bessie smiled. She glanced down at her folded hands.

'I'm sure he would. He'll be getting a bit before the evening's out.'

The tired, comfortable voices grew fainter as I went down the hall. I crossed the lane to Mrs Howard's. Nana's head was near a window, reading. She must have heard me for she looked out and smiled, then turned away from me to tell the Little Woman I was coming.

It was dark when we got home, but I knew the stairs so well I could climb them two at a time. I told mother granny was coming up. She already had a fire lighting in the little room.

All together, granny and mother and Maggie were talking about Dalkey. There was a country perfume of flowers that Mrs Howard had given me. In the lamplight they were a blaze of colours. Fresh from Dalkey — there was no place like Dalkey. 'And the Mazie is looking better,' mother said. 'She's like a two-year-old.'

'Do you know what I did,' said granny, plonking down in her armchair, 'one of the days? I sang "The Croppy Boy" — would you credit that? I'm dying for a cup of tea.'

Meg and Joe and Kevin all came in to see Nana. The talk grew so loudly excited that Maggie shushed them. 'What will Mutt below think?' When she was disturbed she gave a short cough, twice repeated. It grew quiet enough to hear her give her little cough; then she said quietly to mother,

91

pointing to the door: 'You'd better go and get the tea. There's an apple-pie here in the parcel, that Bessie sent you.'

Of course mother was delighted to hear that Bessie had been asking after her. Mother, pouring our tea, asked after the Little Woman, and wanted to know every detail of what she'd said: 'The Little Woman has great heart — and always had.'

It was the row between Bessie and uncle Joe that roused the most eager and excited talk, though in a guarded manner because walls have ears. The coolness and the fighting going on in Dalkey gave much satisfaction; it was a sort of consolation to know that other people — even in a lovely country place like Dalkey — had their troubles too.

Why the Headmaster
was Great

At school English lessons were the best, but also we had to do Irish. The boy who was good at Irish gave out the copy-books. We sat two to a desk, and each desk had its inkwell sunk into a hole and a brass flat cover you could slide back.

With faces held close to our copy-books, pens gripped in tight inky fingers, we slowly copied out the Irish alphabet. Dipping into the white delph inkwell, I shaped an Irish *A*, like a steep roof seen sideways on a curving base — an Irish harp upside down! The Irish letters were more squiggly than the English, and different, like the Irish *G* that was a skinny *S* with a flat top.

A bonus with these writing lessons was the smell of the ink. I was too nervous to enjoy it properly because the bitter-sweet perfume of the blue-black ink was so mixed up with school.

After prayers one morning a shock awaited me. When the folding partitions had been closed and Mr O'Neill had gone away, Mr McManus pointed at me with his finger and said loudly: 'O'Beirne, you are to go to Mr O'Neill's room.'

'Yes, sir.' I was faint with nervousness, caused by a secret guilt. I had memorised the first page of the Irish book without understanding a word of it. Mr McManus in some strange way, I thought, had found me out and only the headmaster could punish me enough for cheating.

There was a lady teacher in Mr O'Neill's room, from the Infants' School downstairs. Mr O'Neill was just sitting there, twisting one end of his moustache.

'Come here, boy,' he said, jerking his head to beckon me over. 'I want you to take this pen and show us how you make an Irish *A*.'

I saw my Irish copy-book on his desk. Wondering, I took the pen and did as I was told.

'Excellent!' the lady teacher said. 'Excellent — do it again.'

Both of them leaned forward, watching closely as I made another Irish *A* and then another, with casual ease. The attention they gave me was delightful and very puzzling.

'Most interesting,' the teacher said. 'An Irish *A* can be written perfectly without lifting the pen — this boy can do it.' Mr O'Neill nodded. The lady said I was a very neat writer. Then she made an Irish *A* as I had done, without lifting the pen. 'Thank you,' she said, and went out smiling.

Mr O'Neill turned his chair around and stared at me.

'Do you like Irish, boy?'

I said: 'No.'

He thought for a moment, leaning back.

'Tell me, have you done any drawing?'

'No, sir.'

'H'm.' Mr O'Neill rubbed his cheek with his finger-tips. 'You are fond of reading, I expect?'

'Yes, sir.' I added, beginning to enjoy the conversation: 'I read a lot now. One of the books I've read was called *A Christmas Carol.*'

'Ah yes, Charles Dickens. I like reading myself. In fact,' he said, smiling a nod of regret, 'it's about the only relaxation I have. Tell me, have you read this new novel, *The Wings of a Dove?*'

'No, sir. Not yet.'

'Hmmmm.' There was a pause, while Mr O'Neill frowned thoughtfully. He turned his pince-nez full upon me.

'I'm just wondering... would you care to do some extra work, at home? I don't mean as part of your home exercise. This would be special work, for me.'

'Yes I would. I'd love to, sir.'

He stood up and walked across the room to a glass-fronted cupboard. I took a book full of blank pages from him, and a pencil.

'I'm giving you this drawing book,' Mr O'Neill said. 'Bring me a drawing every morning. Or as often as you can. I think you will find it interesting — only choose something simple to draw first, like a chair or a clock. Something easy, to begin with.'

'Thank you, sir.'

The book with its blue cover, and the pencil, felt enormous as I carried them back to my desk. I could feel excitement pounding in my head.

Mr McManus should be told what had happened. Only he was busy, writing sums on the blackboard. Perhaps I could tell Ronan, sitting here beside me? He might only think I was boasting. The whole affair seemed so peculiar and so odd that for the time being it would be best, I decided, not to make a big thing out of it.

Nevertheless I knew in myself a feeling of importance, and of pride. Mr O'Neill was great. I would do my very best for him, would bring him splendid drawings and he would be glad he helped me.

At home my mother was the first to be told about the great event. I was being taught to be an artist, I explained, choking down my dinner. Mother said to go into the little room and show granny the nice book, and I could draw away in there.

I hurried to granny's room and turned the brass knob, but the door was locked. I knew from previous similar occasions that granny had gone to Miss White, because when that happened she always made sure to lock the door. I waited, for she was never very long; and sure enough I heard the key turn in the lock and I was able to go in.

It made all the difference these evenings having David to go out and play with. He might finish his home ekker early and come politely to the door, and knock. Or I might rush down, and around by Moffey's Corner to grip the railings and call to the blank area below with its barred windows: 'David!' If he didn't come out at once I would give a shrill whistle. He would appear gazing up, a hand shielding his eyes to see me better against the bright sky. 'I'll be up in a sec!' he would call.

Sometimes other boys played with us, including my brother Joe. I was at a disadvantage in running games as I always had to wear my overcoat to hide a patch on my trousers. Even at school I wore the overcoat, and admired all the more David's fine dark blue suit. Mother said she would get one like it for my Confirmation.

David and I had long outgrown the tame Duke's Lawn, and even Stephen's Green. We adventured along the banks of the Grand Canal, and soon like other big boys we were fishing with nets on bamboo sticks. We got to know the dark stillness beneath several bridges, black, terrifying depths where the banks were concrete, and wide, grassy shallows where the reeds were growing. Once I caught a real fierce-looking stickleback, as long as your finger.

I was allowed down to see David's black rabbit, in the back garden. David knew where the pet-shop was and would come with me when I had two shillings, he promised.

Dr Horne had his garage at the back of our house, and this back yard was always deserted. I could put my hutch on a little sloped roof down there. The hutch was a butter-box. It had a back entrance that could be fastened and I nailed wooden bars across the front.

All this time I did drawings for Mr O'Neill along with my home ekker, but the rabbit was something that had to be dealt with as well. David and I walked half across the city to an old-fashioned part beside St Patrick's church. There was a bird market there, up an entire wall of cages on Sundays, David said.

We passed Johnnie Fox's in Bride Street, where you could buy everything in the world, and came to this window full of birds and rabbits and white mice. Inside the shop there was an uproar of birds, budgies, and parrots, even a monkey chattering. An old lady came forward to see what we wanted.

'Yes?'

'How much are the rabbits, please?'

'Two shillings.'

'I'll take one,' I said promptly. 'Black, if possible.'

Kicking, held brutally by his ears, a black, glossy-coated rabbit was handed indifferently across the counter. I tucked him under my overcoat. I remember thinking how incredibly cheap he was — a live black rabbit!

All the way home he kept nosing further and further into the dark recesses of my coat, but at last, with relief and joy, I saw him like a living shadow safely behind bars. He had wood-shavings to sleep on, and a supper of cabbage-leaves and bread and water.

When I brought down fresh cabbage-leaves next morning, shrewdly avoiding Miss O'Leary, I found the bars gnawed though and Blackie gone! I searched all down Clare Lane, around Lincoln Place, everywhere, and to make it worse, mother said 'I'm glad that unlucky thing is gone.'

I was late for school — the first time ever — and had to line up with other 'lates' in the headmaster's room for punishment. It was the room to which I came each morning with my drawing, standing apart, if sympathetically, from the dejected line of late arrivals. This morning I was one of them.

It made me feel twice as awkward now, because Mr O'Neill had been so friendly. There was something peculiarly humiliating about being deliberately slapped at any time, but Mr O'Neill and me being friends made it impossible. Surely he would let me off? He drew the strap from his hip-pocket almost absently and glared at me — first of the line — and snapped: 'Hold out your hand, boy!' I felt sure our eyes could never meet again.

Mr O'Neill, however, didn't seem to mind. Soon afterwards he was gazing at my drawing, twirling his moustache and rubbing the ends upward with his fingertips. 'Yes, this is quite good,' he said, 'except for the hair on the man's head.' Making strokes with a pencil he showed me how to draw hair, and while he was at it, how to draw a man's eye so that it looked alive. 'See that?' he said. 'Now that's more like it. If it's all black it simply looks like a black eye.'

This was the day of the fight. The other boy was tough, vindictive-looking, with a bony face. It came as a surprise to me that the entire school suddenly expected us to fight, and there was no escape. It was to be around the corner in Sandwith Street as soon as we got out. These fights were occasional events that never failed to arouse intense excitement.

From the moment I heard 'fight' and knew that it meant me, I thought of it uneasily, hoping that the other boy would go on home. There seemed to be no chance of that. As we were nearing the gate the crowd of boys behind kept pushing me. Those already in the street set up a roar: 'Come on! A fight! A fight!' A drove of boys crushed through the gateway and the noise was deafening.

Cheering and shouting, the crowd was like a river roaring past the school to swirl around the nearby corner where a whirlpool formed and I saw faces all staring at me. One was Ronan's, and he seemed pale. I began to feel sick inside and my legs were trembling. I tried to smile at Ronan but my lips felt tight, then the tightness was making my throat dry.

How could the fight ever start? I saw the other boy in front of me but I had no wish to hit him. He kept sparring — all the faces roared. The faces vanished in a jagged blackness, a shattered picture. My nose seemed to be flattened into one bitter-tasting, rhythmic throb.

Blinking tears away, I saw him. He was sparring, and he kept staring at me with his vicious grin. He bobbed up and down, fists ready, shouting: 'Come on!' I ground my teeth and ran at him with arms whirling but he fell back — back and back into the crowd. I hated him. I saw his bony face take on a startled expression. He was frightened! He had turned his back on me and was running, but amazingly all the others were running as well!

I stood gaping after them. As I gaped a wet, smelly, chilly thing slapped into my face. It was a dishcloth. 'Get along home, yous lot of dirty little bastards!' screamed a woman who had darted from her house and was lashing out in all directions. So all fled in consternation — and in my case, with heartfelt relief.

My drawing the following morning was of a grim-faced cowboy, not unlike the film star William S. Hart, pointing his pistol at Mr O'Neill.

'H'm. You've been in a fight,' the headmaster said. 'I see you've got yourself a black eye.'

'It wasn't the other fellow gave it to me, sir,' I said quickly. 'It was a woman with a dishcloth — with a button on it.'

He smiled to himself and rubbed his chin, gazing with little or no interest at William S. Hart. I'd gone to a lot of trouble with that drawing, and when I was doing it even the corners of my own lips, I noticed, had been curled down in a kind of snarl.

'I didn't want to fight him, sir,' I said. 'I was glad the woman came and ran us.'

'Billo', as we boys called him privately, had a good laugh at that.

My Father Hears
Home Truths

It came finally to Confirmation Day, a murky, drizzly morning. I had dreaded this day and yet looked forward to it, for it was the day I was to wear my new blue suit.

In the mirror I looked splendid in my new shirt and tie and the firm, clear-cut jacket. But the cloud-filled window was ominous. Buttoned into the stiff, transforming suit that even smelled new I sat on the edge of a chair, too dejected to speak. Glumly gazing down at my nicely-creased short trousers, the beautiful smooth suit, the red silk ribbon with its medal on my darkly crisp lapel, I knew that all this glory must be hidden under my old overcoat.

What would the fellows think if I went out in my new suit in the rain? They knew I had an overcoat. I'd worn it every day, and they would say, so why not now? They'd surely imagine I was showing off. At last, with the overcoat unbuttoned to display my medal I set off in the rain to be confirmed.

The question I was asked was dead easy, 'Who made the world?' Everyone knew that, without having to learn a lot of catechism. A wrinkled, ringed hand came forward near my face and I kissed it.

On the way home I fingered the money in my trousers pocket, wondering what to buy. From the counter in McCarthy's I picked up a little comic like a book, the *Nelson Lee*. I'd never noticed it before, but now it would become the comic I liked best of all. The stories were all about Nipper, who was head of the Fourth, and who helped the athletic housemaster-detective, Nelson Lee, to solve some fantastic criminal cases. These tales of school life and crime were all written by the same man, Edwy Searles Brooks. He was the best-ever school story writer.

All that afternoon I sat hunched over the little pages, reading how petticoat rule threatened the school, and led to the exciting events of this week's tale, 'The Great Barring-Out'. Nipper and his pals had built a barricade, and the cover-picture showed a spiteful-faced lady teacher recoiling from a jet of water gushing from a hose pointed straight at her! Meanwhile a crime had taken place and Nelson Lee was on the track. But the door opened, and my brother Joe came into Nana's room.

I heard my granny saying, in a rather annoyed tone — for she thought Joe very bold: 'And to what do we owe the pleasure of this visit, pray?'

Joe stared at me.

'*He* wants you, Michael,' he said, and went out leaving the door ajar.

I walked along the lobby after Joe, neither slowly nor quickly, just like normal. He had never sent for me like this, so I wondered what was up and felt slightly frightened going into the Far Room. My father had finished his dinner and was sitting with his feet up on a wooden settee at the window.

Suddenly I remembered that I was wearing my new suit. He was looking at me with a nervy tremor in his eyes, and he gave a kind of smile. Against the day-bright window his head looked bald in front, above his deep-ridged forehead.

'Show your new suit, Michael!' mother exclaimed.

He put a hand out to feel the sleeve.

'May you have long life to wear it,' he said. 'Turn around.' I turned obediently, and turned back facing him, feeling at ease.

'So today was your Confirmation.'

'Yes.'

'What did he ask you?'

'Who made the world?'

'And you knew the answer, I bet.'

'Yes. God made the world.'

'Here, I suppose you'll be wanting a few sweets and comics.' He held out a fist to me. 'Put that in your pocket for hansel. I'm a bit shook, but sure you may as well have it as the bookie.'

It was two half-crowns he gave me. He got good money in the Corporation on account of having a trade.

'Thanks very much.' I felt a grateful glow. I was giving weekly payments off a concertina — a concertina with a tutor — and the unexpected money brought it nearer. Moved by a friendly impulse, I said: 'This is a book I got today, Mister. Did you ever read it?'

With an easy, lazy grip my father took the *Nelson Lee*. He had a cigarette in his left hand, smouldering, but he thumbed back a curve of pages. He let them flip back so that he could see the cover. He really stared at it. I thought he had forgotten I was there beside him.

'This is a novel, Mick,' he said at last. 'That's what it is, a novel.' I noted, with a surge of joy, that he had turned to the beginning of the story. It was an opportunity I grabbed eagerly.

'Would you like to read me a bit, Mister?'

Somehow I knew he would like to. His eyes had that minute quivering. He pushed his shoulder nearer to the window, distrustfully eyeing the print. I held my breath, watching and waiting, aware of my heart beating. He was going to read to me!

The moment he started to read my father's voice changed to a higher pitch. The words followed one another slowly and his finger kept pressing on from word to word. Even though he read slowly, like that, some of the words sounded wrong. A word that came twice in one sentence was 'problem', but he called it 'probable' — 'It was no easy probable, but it was a probable that Nelson Lee must solve.' Which sounded terrible. I could do better than that myself!

My father kept moving his finger across the page and his face went rigid, where he was trying not to yawn.

'This 'ud only make you dopey, Mick,' he said, handing it back.

'Thanks, Mister.' I went to the door and there paused, looking back. 'It's a great story, though, all the same!' I went in to show the *Nelson Lee* to Maggie.

'More horrors!' She pressed her hands into her lap and hunched her shoulders, pretending to shiver. Then she went on reading her own book, Zane Grey's *Riders of the Purple Sage*.

Everyday life could be boring — on Sundays especially — and that was why people read novels. There'd surely be a bit of excitement in a story. Yet everyday life could be exciting too, unexpected things happening, the voice of a newsboy fading into the distance repeating, ever fainter and fainter: 'Stop Press!' Terrible things like bombings and fires and murders happened every day.

Even the best of stories, though, lacked the glamour of real life in our school when things were going well. School didn't seem so bad at all as we moved up to Third, then up to Fourth, with Mr McManus, happily, still with us.

When you were actually there in your desk — I had Ronan beside me — and the folding partitions had been closed around the room, it was all right. Mr McManus was teaching us how to pronounce words like 'interested' and 'suitable' and 'massacre'. When one of us heard that our master was an M.A. the whole class felt proud, without knowing exactly why.

It sometimes happened that Mr McManus would saunter forward from the blackboard eyeing the class shrewdly. Then, without any particular reason, he would begin to talk. Hitching up a well-pressed trouser-leg to sit on one of the front desks he would begin chatting to the boy who was good at Irish, and the talk would spread. It was up to us to prolong the friendly respite by asking questions. Only the strap flicking beneath our master's bent knee reminded us of grimmer moments.

Mr McManus used to talk about his digs.

'Ah, you don't know how lucky you are,' he'd say smiling, rubbing the side of his nose. 'You have your mothers to look after you.'

'No place like home, sir!'

That impudent comment sounded shocking. It drew a frown of reproof, and in the silence we feared that our master would refuse to be cajoled. However, we were in luck.

'But when you are in digs, as I am,' Mr McManus said, flicking at his trouser-leg, 'things are different. The landladies don't seem to use their head. They'll cut up half a loaf and leave it there, buttered, day after day. It never seems to occur to them to leave the loaf, so that one could cut and butter it oneself, at meal-times.'

A voice from the back bawled: 'Sure you're lucky to get butter at all, sir!'

The master rubbed a reddened cheek, annoyed yet amused too, in spite of himself. 'You mean they'd give me margarine?' he said. 'I don't think so. I'd watch out for that, never fear!'

'Some of them 'ud even go to Boland's Bakery!' a boy shouted. 'You know, sir — with a pillow case, for when the broken bread is gettin' gave out!'

'That will do, Smithers.' Mr McManus turned sideways looking towards the blackboard, about to stand up. Then he turned back and smiled at the class. 'What about the gentleman who lives beneath the three brass balls?'

Whistles of delight shrilled. A hand shot up, rocking for attention: 'Hey! Hey, sir! *Uncle!*'

'Quite right, Fay. That's a popular name for the pawnshop — Uncle's.'

We all laughed. There was fellow-feeling in the fact that everybody knew already. But Smithers was eager to put in his prate again. His hand was up, fingers anxiously snapping: 'Sir! Sir!'

'Well, Smithers?'

'"Aw go on, Mick."' Smithers mimicked, '"have a heart, give us the fifteen bob!" And — and "Gent's blue in white," sir!'

'Attention!' The master stood up; the magic moments turned matter-

102

of-fact. It was time for the next lesson.

After school I sometimes hurried to Westland Row corner and crossed by the cab-rank with its line of dejected, blinkered horses, into the upper part of South Great Brunswick Street. It meant only a slight detour from the usual way home, but these were mere sentimental journeys. My objective was always the same shop-window outside which I could brood sadly before turning reluctantly away.

In any case, this part of Brunswick Street was hallowed ground. Even gazing in the window I was conscious of the opposite side, where stood the Palace Cinema, the Penny Rush where we kids crowded in for the Saturday matinees. The inside, crammed with wooden benches, would be inky black until vaguely illuminated from the screen. That was when the piano struck up and — to a burst of cheering — there appeared a large white oblong grained with silver rain.

This was our world of galloping horses, broad-brimmed sombreros and smoking six-shooters. The big picture featured William S. Hart, Buck Jones, or Tom Mix galloping up and down rugged mountains in trails of dust and leaping across gaping canyons, all out to save the girl. Intelligent, helpful horses were Silver and Trigger, and the screen hero of all dogs, Rin-Tin-Tin, also played his part to foil the villains.

Whenever the film broke or the projector jammed, replacing high adventure with a blank white screen, there'd be the crash of stamping feet and cries of 'Show the picture!' We were an impatient, excitable lot. We really got right into those movies, and often there were frenzied shouts: 'Go on, the chap!' or the urgent warning: 'Look behind you!'

But it was the 'folly-ups' that truly got us. Not even the Queen's Theatre further up the street, with its plays and pantos and Power and Benden turns could compare with 'folly-ups' for sheer intensity. Even today I feel a sense of awe and horror as I see again, walled in by unscalable cliffs, a pond of sinister, dark water — The Bottomless Pool.

Bottomless. One Saturday Pearl White fell into this nightmare trap. The villain, Elmo, was limping after her at great speed in his flowing black cloak. To avoid his evil clutches Pearl dashed to the brink of The Bottomless Pool, and jumped in. There she was now, swimming round and round with no chance of escape, *To be continued at this Theatre Next Week*.

Of late, however, I had developed this other interest, more serious than any 'folly-ups'. Unfailingly each Saturday I entered the large huckster-shop owned by the Misses O'Grady, the very shop outside which I stood now, to gaze raptly in the window. My concertina with tutor was in there, waiting.

Overleaf: IRA gunmen in Dublin, 1922.

On Saturdays I could enter the shop boldly and hand my two shillings up over the counter to one of the Miss O'Gradys. They were exactly alike in appearance. They were tall, shadowy-grey ladies with haughty bitter-sweet faces clouded by wisps of grey hair, and it didn't matter which of them took the two shillings.

I knew that the concertina and tutor, in its box, would be handed down from the high counter the very moment my final payment had been made. The longed-for moment might not be till Christmas, but by now Christmas was a real possibility, already talked about at home.

But a mournful event intervened.

On a blustery November evening David Hassett told me that his family would be moving. It was to happen that very week, and they would go to a far-away place on the north side of the city, Inchicore. I took a note of David's new address, without much hope of ever seeing him again. We parted with a stoical 'So long'.

For me it was a tragic parting. It meant I had no friend. At school there was Ronan, of course, a good friend but strictly a school friend, who lived away somewhere remote with his grandmother.

There was nothing for it but to settle down every evening with my drawing, my home ekker and my comics. I often bought a Buffalo Bill comic, not to read but for the cover picture, which I would copy and some-times even paint in colour.

It was only for Mr O'Neill that I bothered with drawings at all. Enthus-iasm lagged — though when you were drawing a face it wasn't bad: corners of lips turned down sourly, the eyes like mere slits, the six-shooter smoking.

When Maggie came in from work I'd still be at it. I was a little bit afraid of Maggie. Of late she had been in especially grumpy moods, and she had a bitter tongue. She was tight-lipped this evening, too.

There was still some brightness up to half-past eight. When it began to get dark my aunt moved nearer to the window and continued reading to herself. Nana was in bed. Sometimes Maggie's lips would mutter.

Suddenly she snapped at me: 'Have you no sense at all? Can't you see you're in your own light! Face the window!'

My picture looked good. I was painting in the last part, consisting of sky and white clouds. Dipping my brush in blue, I scarcely noticed the staccato outburst like a car back-firing in the distance. I knew what it was, the Sinn Feiners and the English were still fighting. These noises would always die away as they did now. A military lorry roared past and the street fell silent.

'It's not finished yet!' my aunt said, half to herself. I felt less tense — glad that the shooting had distracted her from being so glum.

Granny had been fairly sick for weeks. She lay in the bed, raised up against two pillows, and in the gathering dusk her small, curve-nosed face was very still. She had fallen asleep while I'd been painting. But the pillows shifted and she wakened, falling sideways with a cry of alarm.

'Musha, why can't you be more careful,' Maggie said reproachfully, getting up to fix the pillows. 'Anyone would think you were a child!'

'I must have dozed off,' granny said.

'Dozed off!' Maggie repeated with scorn. 'So after being in bed all day you must doze off! You'd try the patience of a saint.'

'Oh dear! I wonder you never give that tongue of yours a rest,' granny said testily. 'Morning to night it's nag, nag, nag!'

'What's that?' my aunt said, without moving.

I heard a crash. The floor shook. From the far room a shivering scream rang out.

'Merciful God!'

Maggie sprang to the door, wrenched it open and was gone. The floor shook again as I ran after her along the lobby. I felt sick with fear and shock. It was dark. I could hear my father shouting, cursing. There was another scream as I reached the door of the far room. I saw my mother falling. My father was in shirt sleeves, rolled above his elbows. He stood in the dark room and my aunt stood in the doorway. I came up beside her. My father strode forward, broken plates on the floor cracking under his feet. 'Get out!' he shouted. 'Get out, the lot of yous!'

Grim-faced, glaring at him, Maggie stood her ground. He made as if to shove her roughly but my mother pushed her way between them. Mother had hurried past us, gasping; she crouched rigid by the bedroom door. 'Here Michael — come here!' she cried. 'Maggie don't speak to him! Don't you stay there!'

She clutched Maggie's arm, but Maggie jerked free of her and faced my father. My aunt was only half his size, yet she looked him up and down, with calm contempt.

'What are you?' she said in a hard, bitter voice. 'Do you call yourself a man?' A pause, then with pent-up venom she lashed out: 'You have a nerve! A thing like you — a nothing, a common corner-boy!'

He shouted: 'I'll wreck the bloody kip! I'll swing for that whore, and you too!'

'There's not a spark of manhood in you,' Maggie said with scorn. 'You'll get a cooling, though I'll see to that!'

107

'Do what you bloody well like!' he shouted. 'Get the police — get to hell out of here! Fuck the lot of yous!'

My father slammed the door.

I was glad of the dark and the sudden silence. All that time, while I had been in Nana's room, the row must have been going on. Now that Maggie had attacked him, her courage made me feel ashamed. In a few more months I'd be eleven, I was taller than Maggie. Had I been there during the row I could have tried to push my father back, I could have stood between them.

It was over now. He was subdued again. I knew by the way he'd said 'Do what you bloody well like!' that he was half afraid. Quietly I went into the bedroom. The others were all sitting there in silence, in the dark.

A Bitter-Sweet
Christmas

It was only a few days to Christmas and I had been shopping. Hurrying home I rushed upstairs with a square cardboard box, stole quietly into the bedroom to be alone, placed the box on a bed. I removed the lid and for the first time really saw my concertina. It was of reddish glossy wood, a compact octagonal shape with leather hand-supports. Carefully prized from its box the concertina relaxed on my knees, stretching itself with a happy little sigh.

Immediately I propped up the tutor and began to practise the first tune, 'Home Sweet Home'. You didn't have to understand a note of music, it showed which button to press: One *Two*, One Two *One*, One Two *One* One, Two, Three, Four. Each button played two different notes, depending on whether you made the concertina suck in air or blow it out. My tutor even gave the words:

'Where e'er—you may—wan—der, there's no—o place—like home;
Be it—ev—er so hum—ble, there's—no—o place—like—home...'

Like my mouth-organ before it, the concertina was not greatly appreciated. Even my mother, always especially gay at a time of full and plenty, lost patience and scolded: 'Oh, for God's sake shut up with that!'

I'd noticed how people at this time could change, and like in *A Christmas Carol*, become good and kind. Of course it was the birthday of the Baby Jesus. Maybe that was why nearly everybody seemed to feel a special glow that made the cold, dark days less dark and cold.

I remember this Christmas Eve well. Miss McCarthy's shop window had all coloured lights around it, and when I went in lots of people were there buying big boxes of chocs and everything. The lights in the shop glittered on a row of frosty Father Christmasses. I'd been sent down for a bar of chocolate but Miss McCarthy said to wait. When the people had gone she stooped under the counter and handed me an oblong box. I knew by its picture that it was a train. She held it towards me.

'For Christmas,' she said, very pleased. Then her face changed. She must have seen that I looked disappointed.

'Oh dear. I'm wrong,' she said. 'That's not for you at all.' She stooped out of sight again and reappeared beaming. 'There's your present!' It was a book called *Prester John,* by John Buchan.

Never before had I been given such a thrilling gift. The title of one chapter was the name of a place in South Africa that was the longest name ever, it went across the page: Blaauwildebeesteafontain. I had read books before, and had listened to books being read out, but never had I known a story quite like this. It seemed too real to be a story. But how could I know whether it was real or not? It must be because I was stupid that I felt so puzzled and frustrated.

'Was Prester John a real man, Maggie?' I said anxiously, coming into the little room on Christmas morning.

'Prester John? Is that the book you got from Miss McCarthy? Look, Mazie.' Maggie held the book up to show the cover — a tall black man in a white robe. 'Wasn't that a nice present she gave him?'

'But was he real, Maggie? A real man?'

She was looking at the cover with her glasses on, reading what it said there in a kind of mutter: 'Prester, another word for priest. He was a legendary figure, king and high-priest in one.'

'What does that mean, Maggie, ledge...?'

'Oh. Legendary means — Oh, it was something that happened long, long ago.'

'But it was real? He was real? Was he *real*, Maggie?'

'Oh, if it happened, I expect he was.'

Doubtfully I looked at granny. From her bed she smiled at me.

'I wish you a happy Christmas, Michael.'

'A happy Christmas, Nana.'

She beckoned me nearer. 'Come here to me.'

I felt a coin pressed in my hand.

'A little something I was saving up for the Black Babies. This time it's for you, Michael.'

I mumbled thanks.

'Look at the crib,' she said. 'Ain't it pretty?' It was on the altar near the door. 'Let you kneel down now, and say a prayer before the crib.'

'Sure I'll be going to Mass.' However I went over and knelt before the tiny figures, the ox and ass, the shepherds, Mary and Joseph and the baby figure with his little upraised arms.

Most of that day I was with Maggie and granny, reading *Prester John*. A fowl hung roasting in front of the fire. My aunt's face was red from bending in the heat, but she was good-humoured. By the time it got dark the fowl was done. Maggie put it on a plate among the rich-smelling dark shapes on the table.

'Will I light the candle or the lamp, Mazie?' Maggie said.

'Light the candle. It's a fine big one.'

The page before me brightened.

They were all laughing and joking in the far room when I went in. Joe was wearing a red paper hat. Mother gave me a large slice of Christmas pudding.

'And what did you get from Santa, Mick?' my father said, turning round from the table.

I told him. Of course I didn't believe in Santa Claus, but it was easy pretending. I'd been telling lies for years, often slipping in a guilty admission, true or false, to make the lie more convincing. I told him what toys Santa had left me. 'And Miss McCarthy gave me this.'

My father put a hand up to his face as if to say 'Excuse me.' He was only putting his cigarette in his mouth, head tilted back, half closing his eyes against the smoke. He took the book in his hands. I saw his dark-brown thumb, tobacco-stained, and the blunt, thick nail.

Joe was crouching behind the bed. He had his red paper hat on. 'Lie down!' he kept shouting at Meg. 'You're shot!' Meg refused to be shot. She left off playing with Joe and came over to show me her doll. My smallest brother, Paudeen, was gripping the edge of the table and stepping uncertainly sideways. A cup crashed from the table and he began to cry.

'Be quiet!' my mother said, fixing the kettle on the fire.

Paudeen wailed.

'Come to Daddy,' my father said. 'There, there — come to your Daddy!' He held out his arms.

'Oh, can't you whisht!' mother said to Paudeen, taking him up from the floor. 'He's only frightened. He's all right — there, there! You might cut Michael a bit of pudding, Mister. There, there. Look at that ruffian under the bed! Will you cut Meg a little bit of pudding, Mister.'

After a while I went back to granny's room. *Prester John* was a long story. By the time I had finished it Christmas was well over.

The winter months were punctuated by the crash of Cashel's coal arriving on the outer landing, the various protests of Miss O.Leary about the noise and muddy feet on her stairs, and shouts of 'Stop Press' about tragedies on land and at sea. Looking up at the grey sky we could see millions of dark grey snowflakes falling slowly, whitening the roofs and street and railings.

One Saturday my aunt came home late for her dinner, hours late. I was sure she had been over to Moore Street, but she had no parcels and her face looked sad. I heard her telling Nana that my uncle Paddy who had let me listen to his watch and who had held me on his knee, was dead.

I had heard of people being dead, the faithful departed. At Mass the priest would read out the names of the souls of the faithful departed, saying 'May they rest in peace.' Now death was brought home to me by Maggie with her gloomy face.

'Poor Paddy!' Fingering her oblong leather handbag my aunt sat down with her hat and coat on; she was jaded. 'I could see it in his face last Tuesday, and I across in York Street.'

'Week after week you went there,' Nana said. 'I don't know why — and on an empty stomach.'

But mournfully Maggie went on: ' "How are you this evening, Paddy?" says I looking cheerful. You know. Trying to put a bit of heart in him. "How are you, Paddy?" And he turned on me. "Much you care," he says, "how I am. I'm sure you're frettin." With that he turned his face to the wall, and that's always considered a bad sign. Poor Paddy!' She sighed. 'He was the flower of the flock.'

'It's the good are taken,' Nana said. But she was good, and she was old — not taken yet.

My father brought me with him to see Paddy on Sunday morning. We went up the wide stairways, very hushed, to Roseanna's room. There was a smell as if wine had been spilt, yet acidy too. The bed, the pillow and the sheet were spotless. He didn't look like Paddy. He had big black bushy eyebrows and a black moustache, his face white as the pillow and his thin, dark nostrils jutting up. He was in his brown Third Order habit, like a marble figure on the bed with marble fingers twined around his beads and crucifix.

'God between us and all harm,' my father whispered, tapping his chest with a little 'bless yourself'.

'Kneel down and say a prayer,' Roseanna told us.

At home I felt deeply impressed, remembering Paddy dead. It was a very still, sad Sunday. When it was evening I stood gazing out from Nana's window at the street of houses opposite, all tinged by the sad, sunset glow.

I was glad of the bustling, racketty weekdays with everybody in a hurry somewhere, and I looking forward to the *Nelson Lee*. Nipper, Handforth

112

and the others were like friends, or at any rate people I knew and liked well. It said that in the coming summer Mr Lee would be taking his class abroad to explore the Great Wall of China. You could depend on something special happening every week.

For me a special day was Friday, when I went down to Greene's post-office for the granny's old age pension. The young post-mistress who had been there forty years counted the coins to me briskly after banging her stamp. Another event, sometimes, would be Saturday night with mother across town, on the look-out for a lovely bit of corned beef for Sunday. 'It's better to have it in you than on you,' she'd say, as we came home laden in the tram.

All these things were only trifles compared to what happened to me one Monday, at school. Our English readers had been put away. Copy-books were out for the next part of the lesson, English composition, my favourite subject. Nearly all the fellows hated doing comps the way I hated sums.

'Ireland, my own country' was the subject. A grim silence closed over the class-room, fellows were nibbling their pens, dog-earing their copy-books. I simply dipped pen in ink, thought of the map of Ireland, its mountains and seas, lakes and rivers, and having made a beginning wrote on steadily.

I was reading over what I had written when a hand crossed my line of vision. Mr McManus had been moving quietly among the desks, and just when I'd finished my comp I saw the master's grey sleeve and big white cuff, and his hand out grasping. 'Excuse me,' he said, and he took my copy-book away.

Our master had a sedate yet free-and-easy manner. He had a fresh, healthy complexion, a long upper lip, fierce eyebrows. He would some-times be chewing some white stuff — I think chewing-gum. Then when we'd be working on some lesson he'd put his hands in his trousers' pockets, stare down at his shiny brown shoes, and take a stroll over to Beaver for a chat.

When Mr McManus took my copy-book I felt a glow of pleasure. I knew he thought me good at English and I hoped he would like my comp. With pride I remembered the opening sentence: 'Nature holds Ireland, as it were, in the hollow of her hand.' The thing petered out after that, but I could see that my copy-book with Mr McManus holding it was moving sedately across our class-room and the other class-room, to Beaver at the top.

I saw Mr McManus pointing to the page, and Beaver looking carefully, and nodding. Then Beaver deliberately stared across at me, I thought —

unless he was just staring into space.

I experienced a sort of elation, but it was fragile as a puff-ball the wind whirls away. The comp I had written left Mr McManus and Beaver impressed. When all the copies had been collected Mr McManus read my comp out to the class. Though it wasn't all that wonderful the other boys listened in silence to the master's beautiful enunciation of my words, and they were obviously impressed. The entire class was impressed, but not half as much as I was.

Here was something I had always longed for — recognition; it should have been the biggest day of my life so far. A success like this might have comforted, closed me into a private glow of satisfaction all that day. The trouble was it seemed dreamlike, too lovely to be real; and right enough it was all gone in a minute as we settled down, grimly, to another Irish lesson.

Nevertheless I now took a quiet pride in those words, and their punctuation, that 'Nature holds Ireland, as it were, in the hollow of her hand.' Whatever that sentence might mean it was all my own work, it had been noticed and praised; so I gratefully enshrined it in memory.

The Person
on the
Stairs

I suppose I was on my guard against life, and against big people especially. You could never be sure what big people were going to do next. Coming in the hall-door it made me uneasy to think that Miss O'Leary might pop out and grab me. Then, going up the stairs, there was always the chance that I would meet Mutt coming down, so quiet, so gentlemanly, with his briefly-glancing, sad brown eyes. He was very tall, sort of handsome; he never spoke a word, yet I feared he would suddenly turn on me.

All the same you could have too much peace and quiet, like on Sundays. Weekdays were better. But even then life was not perfect, because every day and everywhere, in Dalkey, in York Street, in Clare Street, in Sackville Street, in Stephen's Green, there was a chance that trouble would flare up — even at sea the *Lusitania* torpedoed with 1,500 souls on board, all drowned. Life seemed to smoulder and erupt with anger, wars, and death.

Even in the *Evening Herald* a kind of fighting was going on every night, between Mutt and Jeff. My granny would get upset about it and cry: 'Oh, for shame! He's a proper ruffian that fellow — the big fellow, what's his name, Mutt. It shouldn't be allowed, the things he does to Jeff.'

Maggie only laughed. She thought Mutt and Jeff were funny, and clever as well. 'What ever will they think of next!'

Someone else who looked at Mutt and Jeff — with close attention — was my father. He had heard, somewhere, that if you knew what to look for Mutt and Jeff gave tips. Alas, you had to know the code, something to do with the way they held their hands. The big men, professional punters, all knew it. My father was convinced that if Jeff put his thumb to his nose at Mutt, the favourite horse in tomorrow's big event could be reckoned a dead cert to win.

It had been a great relief to mother when my father started up a boxing club across the town, in Cavendish Row, because at least it would get him out of the house every night. My father's trainer, the Dicky Bird, was in it and a Jewman named Mo Green, a great sport, had an interest in it, but the outcome of this club was that a great change came over the Far Room that autumn.

Months before, when the club was beginning, my father used to be up half the night at his bench, barking and coughing, sawing and hammering, and Miss O'Leary up hammering in tune with him on the cross door. I think he took a delight in drowning her agitated knocking with a specially loud *crash! crash!* of his mallet: he was making a great circular platform for the club.

Once or twice Mutt knocked on the ceiling of his room — Knock, Knock — with the sweeping-brush or maybe his umbrella, but to no avail. He even came out on his landing one night and called up, in a genteel way: 'Please stop that noise!'

My father opened the cross door and shouted down at Mutt: 'You're nothing but a bloody shaper!' Mutt used to really get his rag out — 'A fellow that's only living on his wits!' my father shouted. 'A fellow that never worked and never will!'

He went back to his bench and his hammering. Nobody was going to stop or interfere with *him*!

One autumn evening long after this my father came home as usual and was in his shirt sleeves by the fire, going over the horses he done with the *Final Buff Mail*, when there was a knock on the cross door. I was told to answer it. Along the lobby came the Dicky Bird, a little cheerful sandy man, a great whistler and admirer of my father's ring-craft, who had even gone up to Belfast for the semi-finals.

'Well, Jem,' the Dicky Bird said, putting a hand on my shoulder, 'are you going to be a champ like your father?' I muttered that my name wasn't Jem, and I was saying 'No', but he was all talk to my father, so mother beckoned us children out into the other room where the baby was asleep. You could still hear the moo, moo of them talking.

The two of them were talking inside about the boxing club in Cavendish Row. There had been trouble over there, it seemed. They had nearly come to blows, the three of them, in this big row in Cavendish Row, and Moses Green the Jewman was after taking nearly all the things in lieu of interest. So on the following night, the Friday, here had come the Dicky Bird to talk things over.

About five the next evening, Saturday, my father and the Dicky Bird came all the way over from Cavendish Row on a tram, with two trunkloads of boxing gloves and knicks and bottles of hartshorn and turpentine, and this great platform. We were gazing out when the tram stopped, and saw them getting off on the opposite side. My father and the Bird were almost totally eclipsed by the platform when they stood it on end, like a full moon. It was a special wooden thing made by my father for the punch-ball.

'Ignore the person on the stairs,' my father said as they banged their way up with the awkward, slithering platform and two heavy trunks. Miss O'Leary had seen them. She stood in the hall first, with a ferocious face, grey hair stuck out wild from her bonnet, to prevent them coming up. She went in front of them backwards, one step at a time, till at the turn to the WC she stopped, shouting after them in full scream:

'I'll have the police on yous! Let them not imagine they can turn my house into a common tenement — them and their big tables brought in! The scum and dirt of Dublin! Aaahhh! it's out they'll be going — out, out, out!'

'Who's that oul geezer?' the Dicky Bird asked breathlessly; but they were fairly safe by now, on our own landing. 'A pity about her!' my father said as he shouldered open the cross door. Far away downstairs Miss O'Leary retreated behind her partition, having slammed her own door with a vengeance.

Soon enough Miss O'Leary was to emerge again and snort her way up the stairs to our landing. She couldn't have known what great improvements had been going on inside. First, nearly every iota of furniture was shifted out of the far room into the bedroom. Even the bed went, the one Joe and I slept on. The far room with its wooden floor was left bare except for two chairs, a few ornaments on the mantel-piece over the fire, and the platform.

Joe and I stood watching as they fixed up the platform for the punch-ball. That was when Miss O'Leary arrived, because the hammering was really terrible. You'd think it was the Black and Tans raiding the place. Miss O'Leary only made it worse, the way she kicked and hammered with her two fists on the cross door.

Through this bedlam mother moved like a shadow, from the middle room, along the lobby, past his carpenter's bench, and up to our partition spy-hole to peep out. The hammering, from two directions, had brought Maggie out of granny's room onto the lobby, where she stared stupefied at the shaking cross door.

'In the name of God what is happening?' Maggie said. Then, shouting through the uproar: 'Have yous all taken leave of your senses?'

Suddenly the knocking stopped. 'O'Leary will surely get a heart attack,' mother said, peering. 'She's purple in the face.'

Miss O'Leary was resting just then — gathering strength for a real onslaught. There were a few moments of uncanny silence.

In the far room my father had been fitting the punch-ball into its metal swivel. It hung down, pear-shaped. 'This'll give oul O'Leary something to chew on,' he said. He held the ball between his hands to steady it, then stood ready for action, his boxing-gloves clenched. It was amazing. You couldn't see the ball but you could hear it, like the roar of a train in a tunnel, in front of his fists.

Even Miss O'Leary seemed to be taken aback. The peculiar indoor thunder must have startled and dismayed her. She made a partial retreat, slow and reluctant, still hurling back indignant maledictions, but they had dwindled to the dusky depths by the time the Dicky Bird was leaving. 'I'll be off now, so,' the Bird said at the cross door. 'We'll have the lads along on Tuesday for the preliminary opening event.'

'Game ball, mind your step. Wait a minute and I'll get the lamp.'

'Sure I can find my way all right,' the Dicky Bird said, but he waited on the dark landing, beginning to whistle 'The Moon Hath Raised'. My father held aloft the oil-lamp as they descended to the tune of this romantic air in a dance of twisting banisters and shadows.

On the night of Tuesday a fire reddened the hearth, and then, as a match-flame ascended past wallpaper lilies, out bulbed bright white gaslight on the gym in the far room. Draped with a towel in one corner was the basin-stand, with a bucket of water beside it. On high hung the punch-ball and its shadow. A wooden bench ran the length of one wall, where our bed used to be, and the room looked big and bare.

In the middle room our table stood among the beds, where mother and the baby had lain down to keep warm. It was bright and exciting in the new gym. Myself and Joe sat watching the strange men coming in, and being loudly reassured by my father after they had stumbled up the five flights striking matches. He was in his boxing-knicks already and the Dicky Bird stood grinning in an off-white Aran sweater.

A gentleman friend of my father's, a Mr Fleming, had come along just to watch. One of the boxers was a big straw-haired policeman named Tom, and there was a black little fellow called the Chisler. The men, five or six of them, each laid his cap at one end of the bench for sitting on, and they began to strip off all their clothes. It was hard to believe what great long hairy legs they had, straddled out from their shirts, and Tom was wearing the brown Third Order scapulars.

In no time the room was full of pink bodies in shorts, all standing about or skipping in their boxer's elegant kid boots. The Bird was helping one to put on gloves, but my father could tie on his own with his teeth.

'Come on, Hard Chaw.' My father beckoned with a jerk of his thick gloved hand, and the man came over and was told how to hold his left, well out in front of him. My father twisted the man's glove palm down, pushed the elbow higher and stood back admiringly. 'Game ball. Keep it level with the shoulder, left out all the time.'

They began to prance around each other and the whole room quivered. The man kept bobbing, coming and going, his gloves bunched together under watchful eyes. 'Nice footwork,' my father said. A shocking rattle burst from the platform in the corner where Tom had begun hammering the punch-ball. *Thraaaaaahhh!* it went. *Thrraaaaahhhhh-ah-ah!*

Suddenly my father and the other man — the Chisler — were fighting because the Dicky Bird was after saying 'Seconds out!' It was a proper punch-up in the living-room. They were dancing to and fro, and as they danced the gloves went smack-smack against bare bodies. The Chisler hammered my father right across the room and marked him with red blurs.

'Left up — left foot forward,' my father panted, hard pressed, reeling back against my upthrust hand. His back felt wet but I had helped him to stay on his feet. They went on weaving in and out, warily watching as they pranced and circled and punched each other. I could feel a kind of pressure in my ears as the floorboards bounced, and even the window rattled.

Knock, Knock! came from Mutt's room below. Knock, Knock!

They were fighting in earnest; my father hit the Chisler right in the face — smack! — and shouted to him breathlessly: 'Where's your protection?' He meant about keeping your elbow well up, so they stopped for a minute to consider how the left elbow could swing up or swing down to protect the head. 'And don't forget to keep the chin well in — like this.'

As all the men clustered to look, Miss O'Leary's emphatic screeching pierced faintly the unnatural quiet — something about murder and a final warning that she'd call the police. With all the punching and jumping and shaking, Miss O'Leary's knocks and kicks at the cross door had seemed only a mild background disturbance.

'You need never mind that oul one,' Tom the policeman said. 'Believe you me, no legal work arises in this case. She'd have to go to a solicitor; a policeman would only laugh at her, unless in the event of an assault.'

Now that everything was normal the voice of Mutt could be heard calling indignantly: 'Quiet! Quiet, up there, I say!'

'Will you listen to the Gentleman of Leisure,' my father said. 'Goes around in a straw beamer — never done a hand's turn — kid gloves and a walking-stick. Sure he's nothing but a fly-by-night!'

My father and the Dicky Bird got busy giving all the boxers a rub-down. There was a manly smell of sweat mingled with the harsh tang of hartshorn and turpentine. It was wonderful to see the boxers exercising full-length on the floor, and afterwards being rubbed down and massaged. As my father massaged their muscles with the pungent smelly stuff, he kept up a hissing noise, like the carter in the lane did brushing down his horse. Anyway the men seemed to like it. I wished they would all go away, then we could come in and have our tea around the fire.

Finally, holding the oil-lamp to light their way, my father and the club members went tramping down. It must have sounded like an army to Miss O'Leary in behind her partition, and she may have flounced out to see them go. We could hear faintly my father's warning to the men: 'Pay no attention whatsoever to the person on the stairs, proceed as if you never seen her.'

When they had left the room my mother came in and made tea. After being so long in the bedroom her face looked pale and cold and she walked with her head bent, dragging her loose-fitting shoes along the floor. Her hair was not tidy but I caught glimpses of her face, the lips closed firmly. Since their last row my mother had scarcely spoken to my father.

It was depressing. He came back with the oil-lamp and turned out the gas; the light was now more mellow but my mother didn't seem inclined to talk.

'That chancer Kennedy met me and I coming up,' my father said. 'Complained about the noise; I just walked past him. He's nothing but a show-off and a bluffer.'

'Yes, Mister. Sure you're right.'

'Posing as a gentleman — and not a bite in his stomach, I suppose. If that fellow tries to interfere with me again I'll knock his block off! Tell him that if you see him — from me!'

My mother gave no answer. She had carried in the little table and put cups on it, and milk and sugar.

My father said, suddenly: 'Where's the paper, Missus?'

'Where you left it.'

He began to search around. Then he stood staring, his hands hanging down by his sides.

'It's not here. I told you I wanted that paper! You'd better look sharp and get it!' my father said, his voice rising.

Without speaking my mother went into the bedroom. I followed her. I could hear her shoes dragging as she moved about. The street light outside gave the ceiling and the room a dim paleness.

'The old rotter's on for trouble,' she whispered.

She went back to the far room, walking with a deliberately noisy, indifferent step. We had not found the paper. On the fire, which looked small and bright yet cheerless, the kettle puffed out steam. My father sat hunched forward with his hands spread thick-fingered across the glow.

'Your tea's ready.'

'I don't want any tea! Did you get the paper?'

He turned and looked at her. She stood with head down, silent.

'Well get that bloody paper now!'

Each word was a shock. My mother remained at the small-table, neither moving or speaking. My father looked at her, his face darkening with rage.

'You bitch! You'll get that paper or by God, I'll cut your throat! There's nothing safe in the blasted dump but I'll make a change — by God I will!'

My mother turned rapidly and pushed me towards the door. I went out and her shoes came flapping after me into the bedroom. I could hear Joe snoring. The beds were shapeless blurs. He may be sharpening his razor in the other room! I thought, but a hot cup was put in my hands. I sipped the tea and got into bed, and lay there listening.

There was no sound, not even the intermittent noise of lorries in the street. All *that* fighting had ended, anyway; and suddenly we had a Free State now.

The next morning was a fine, sunny morning. I remember it distinctly. I was standing on the corner of the street close to my home; and gazing up the sunny vista narrowing towards Mount Street Bridge, I kept on thinking: Ireland is free! And I thought to myself, I am eleven years of age, and I am walking along a street in Ireland, my own country. And Ireland is free! It was a stirring thought.

Overleaf: The Gresham Hotel, July 1922.

World of Wonder—
and Dismay

We were doing a poem called 'Glen na Smol' that was in the English Reader, when suddenly I got my great idea. It was still only Fourth Class but a well-established Fourth and we would soon be moving on to Fifth. The drawings that Mr O'Neill encouraged me to bring to him each day had whetted my appetite for more attention — then came this idea. It seemed so obvious I wondered that I had not thought of it before. It was daring in a way: I would write, and publish, a school comic of my own!

I had a brand-new copybook, just the thing for stories and poems, and the pictures I would draw to illustrate them. I was eager to begin and waited impatiently for lunch-hour. I told Ronan about my plan and he looked quite excited — it was a kind of news.

Anyone who liked to stay in when the bell went could do so. It was great to be starting my school comic this very day! I opened the copybook, on the cover of which I'd put a scroll around the name *St Andrew's Comic*. With my lunch in one hand and a pen in the other I settled down over the first page. It would be a story. It would begin with action. The chief character, the great detective, Mr Sexton Blake, came running around a corner and gave a piercing whistle, hailing a taxi...

I looked up, gazing into space. Other heads rose up with mine. Mysteriously, silently, an interested audience had gathered!

'What's that you're writing — a story?'

'Yes,' I said, exalted. Some of the boys were from Sixth, big fellows, and they were watching me respectfully. Alas, I was stuck! Deciding to swallow my pride — it was a small word to be stumped by, but an awkward one — I said in a calm, assured tone: 'Can you spell taxi, please?'

They spelled it. I continued with the story, feverishly excited under a pretence of calm. I was writing a story, and the other boys were craning over my shoulders watching, silent and attentive! It was delightful and astonishing; and it was an experience we all shared. We were bewitched by the magic of creation, the novelty of something new.

The magic of creation, how are you! Even as I was writing, with a pretence of energy and purpose, my mind wandered weakly and I knew that the 'story' was all a sham, and like the comic itself, would come to nothing.

There was often a strong smell of kippered herrings when I went home these days, mingling with the wails of the new baby. My father had given up his boxing club, and he was keeping the household money. He used to bring in food such as cheese, pickles, and cooked ham, and lots of kippered herrings. There was a bare look about the table, with only coloured jars and tinned foods on it.

Luckily I felt compelled to do a drawing every evening for Mr O'Neill. It was a helpful interest. If I drew a man on horseback I could hardly sleep that night thinking how lifelike the horse was. I lost myself in shapes and colours — instinctively knowing, nevertheless, that I could never hope to be an artist.

I might wander to the window and stare out, brooding and depressed. Always I seemed to be chopping and changing, getting nowhere, yet longing to feel I had some definite ambition.

The concertina was still a source of wonder, and I sought it out and fondled it. It was almost round, yet not-round; it was excitingly heavy, something that could make great music; and it played whether you pressed in or pulled out. However, it was popular with nobody except myself, so I just left it there. Music was not for me.

On the other hand I was convinced that for true enjoyment, nothing else in life could rival books. Miss McCarthy had lent me *A Study in Scarlet* by Conan Doyle, and I revelled in the masterful intelligence of Mr Sherlock Holmes. 'We see, but we do not observe.' Sitting in the little room I looked up from the book. In future, I must observe!

The lamp was lit. Maggie was reading the paper, one hand held over her eyes, and her back was turned to me. I could just see one watery curve of her glasses with the orange firelight in it.

My aunt stopped reading as a thought struck her, and turned her face to granny in the bed.

'Mazie, do you know what I seen and I coming up the stairs this evening?' she said, and after a brief pause: 'Mutt!'

'Is that so wonderful?' the granny said. 'Isn't he up and down the same stairs all day long?'

'Ah, yes.' Maggie rubbed her black stockings; the fire was warm. Then,

'Ah, yes,' she said. 'Only, this evening he had a woman with him.'

'And he coming up?'

'Exactly,' Maggie said with satisfaction. 'And he coming up.'

'He does have customers,' granny said, 'looking for flats. She must have been one of his customers.'

'Not this one. This was a tall, bony-faced woman in a herring-bone tweet coat,' Maggie said. 'I wouldn't have minded, but they went past his office door — save the mark! — and into his living quarters.'

'Well, that's queer.' The granny pondered. 'Maybe he's after getting married!'

'I wouldn't put it past him. I dare say he'll never see fifty again, but you never can tell with these handsome, stand-offish types.'

'That's it. It's after getting married he is.' Suddenly granny inquired, her glasses glittering with excitement: 'Did you notice — had he a flower in his button-hole?'

'I'm not sure,' Maggie said. 'He kept turned, like, away from me.'

'Well the cleverness of that,' granny said. 'Getting married on the quiet! That man is as cute as a fox.'

Any little bit of news or gossip brightened up the granny, even the doings of missionary priests in far-off Sierra Leone, who had their photos in the *Missionary Annals*. She would question me about school, how I was getting on, and once when reading her favourite paper, the *Irish Catholic*, she said I ought to read the children's part, called 'Kevin's Cosy Corner'.

Impressed by the stories of Sherlock Holmes I had written a story myself — also, oddly enough, about a mastermind of crime detection. Maggie read it to herself and said it wasn't bad at all, and granny, sitting up in the bed, read it through to the end. I didn't think of showing it to mother; really she had no patience for reading, and there was a sort of coolness on at that time with my father.

Kevin, in the *Irish Catholic*, gave a first and second prize each week for children's paintings and stories, and the winning story or essay would be published.

'Why not send your story to "Kevin's Cosy Corner",' granny said. So I did, that very day.

By now I had become accustomed to having no friend, unless you counted Ronan. David Hassett lived so far away that there really was no point in writing to him; he seemed to belong to the past. In any case, in the immediate future my life was to take a new turning.

There was nothing to read. The tuppenny comics you could finish in an evening, so on Sundays I could only miserably mooch around. Maggie said

126

I should join St Teresa's Library in Clarendon Street, which was beside the church. Mr Fleming, the gentleman my father knew, had been up to see him about rejoining the Sodality, so my father now went to this Carmelite church and would be in the way of introducing me.

So one Sunday my father and I went to the Men's Sodality Mass in Clarendon Street. We had to walk on the roadway, so many people were crowding out from Mass, and going in. There was an array of gold-fringed Sodality banners: St Anthony, St Jude, B.V.M. Pray for us, St Dominic, St Francis of Assisi, St Mary Magdalen, and a pungent aroma of incense.

After Mass we stepped across to the library building which had dusty posters on the windows about some faded red EXCURSION. I stood at the counter dejectedly beside my father. The place looked and smelled musty and I felt sure all the books must be religious.

Mr Fleming was there already. Also behind the counter was a tall, golden-haired man who shook hands warmly with my father. He belonged to the Sodality and had only recently come back from America.

My father said, putting a hand on my shoulder: 'This is the eldest, Mick.' I couldn't help twitching my eyebrows angrily. Mr Fleming and the other man both beamed at me as my father went on to say how fond I was of books, and how good I was at the drawing.

'Tell me now,' Mr Fleming said, eyeing me candidly, 'could you draw a cart?'

'Yes, I could.'

He banged the counter, laughing, and winked at my father.

'All right, sonny, have a look around the shelves. You can take any book you like — only be sure to bring it back!'

I found a fairly thick one, with marvellous pictures. It was *Moby Dick.*

'Now you'll enjoy that book,' Mr Fleming said, as he wrote down my name. 'That's a really *good* book. Sure we keep nothing here but what's good!' he added with a shout of laughter, and my father gave a happy grin.

Coming out we crossed the road to Morton's barber-shop, always open on Sunday mornings. Mr Morton was cutting a customer's hair. The air smelled sharp yet moist, with a soapy perfume. The barber was a stocky, red-faced man of fifty who gave the impression he had always been there, just the same, and always would be.

The saloon was full of men reading their Sunday papers. They seemed to talk about racing and football most of the time, and my father knew most of them. 'How're you, Mick!' 'Game ball.'

'We still only charge half-a-crown for a haircut and a shave,' Mr Morton was saying in his grumbly voice, as we came in. 'But did yous ever hear the story about the customer in this swanky joint where the charge was a dollar? Well,' Mr Morton said, snipping away, 'this customer paid up his dollar all right, then he calls the boss over. Well it's terrible hot weather and the place is full of flies. You know.'

Here Mr Morton paused, gazing around the saloon to make sure the story was being listened to. It was.

'Well, the customer says to the boss when he comes over, "Would you like to know a sure way of getting rid of all them flies?" So needless to say, the answer is yes. So your customer says, "You'll never see another fly in your shop if you take my advice, but it'll cost you ten bob."

'The ten bob is paid, the customer goes to the door, and there and then he delivers his advice: A Cure for Flies. "You only have to catch one fly," he says, "by the scruff of the neck, give him a haircut and a shave, and charge him five bob." Goodbye now — and goodbye to all your bloody flies!' Mr Morton gave a screech of a laugh and went on snipping.

I shared in this routine for a couple of Sundays, Mr Morton chatting away as he shaved or trimmed, short back and sides, while the customers waited and listened or read newspapers. My father soon tired of the Sodality and my aunt Maggie took over the visits to church and library.

This library was better than any Aladdin's Cave — a world of the marvellous. I took down from the shelves an austere-looking volume entitled *A Journey to the Centre of the Earth*. The engraved illustrations alone were breath-taking, careful etchings of scenes at the very centre of the earth lit by a sombre terrestrial sun. Jules Verne, Fenimore Cooper, Mayne Reid, Captain Marryat passed through my hands as a succession of wondrous worlds, and St Teresa's Library became my Mecca.

I could see now that the story I had posted off to the *Irish Catholic* was a pitiful poor thing. Even at that time, I sensed that my total lack of confidence would hinder me from ever writing a real story. Yet every Friday, collecting the *Irish Catholic* for Nana, the first thing I looked for was the children's corner.

One Friday, so many weeks had passed I felt sure it must be now or never. In McCarthy's I longed to open Nana's paper. I opened it in the street and there was my story — printed! I saw through tears of joy the title in black letters, and my name beneath. With a dazed feeling, coming into Nana's room, I told her they'd printed my story. It was hard to pretend to be calm.

I let Nana read the story and that evening I showed it to Maggie. Somehow I didn't want her to read it out, like she read out real stories.

She sat aside with her glasses on, reading it; then she looked over to my expectant face and nodded. 'Mind you, it's very good, Michael. And I see they've given you First Prize.' I kept asking if she really thought my story interesting, and patiently she'd answer 'Yes.' At last I decided to take my published effort into the Far Room and let them see it.

As I came to the door it opened; I heard shouting, then my mother fled past me and ran down the stairs. She was screaming for help, running down to the street. I could hear my father shouting and cursing inside, and the children came out; Joe, Meg, Kevin, Paudeen, straggled along the lobby with frightened and bewildered faces.

Quickly and quietly Maggie came forward and took the trembling children into Nana's room. I rushed down the stairs after my mother. At the hall-door, I saw her coming, very small, without her hat or coat on, with a policeman.

The two of them went into the Far Room. I heard my father's voice raised angrily and went in after them. The door stood open. The policeman had his helmet under one arm and he was sitting on the bed. I stared at my father but he didn't see me, he was glaring like a wild man.

My father talked rapidly, standing there with shirt-sleeves flapping and hands going in agitated gestures. The fire blazed cheerily. Against her white face my mother's eyes were like burnt dots. All seemed small and ordinary compared to the enormous policeman with the dark uniform and gleaming helmet. Slowly he drew out his notebook, asking questions, though he wrote nothing down. By now the row seemed trivial. 'Did he threaten you?' the policeman kept repeating. To judge by what mother said, my father had attacked her with a razor. All the voices had sunk to a low monotone, without anger, there being nothing left except the miserable explanations.

'She's going to ask for a separation,' my aunt said, coming in at last to Nana who was sitting up against the pillows. 'She's in the bedroom with the children and he's asked her to make tea. That man can't be in his right mind!'

This latest outburst had been worse than former rows. There was tension, a feeling that something different must happen now. We sensed a big change coming, but what would our lives be like then?

Fancy Free

Joe was to be a witness, he having been there when it happened. The morning they were going to court my mother got ready early and looked smart and fresh; she even had new stockings. The last I saw she was licking the pill-box to moisten it, and reddening her cheeks.

When I came in from school that evening mother and Joe had only just arrived back. They were in the little room, all talk with Nana. Mother greeted me with a glad smile.

'I got my separation, Michael — we're in town! Now we'll all have a nice cup of tea, I'm only wall-fallin'.'

'Was *he* there?' I asked.

'Was he there? Sure, wasn't he up in the witness-box! And he like a real old man, with hair sticking out from the baldy pate over his two ears. He was more like something wild you'd meet.'

Soon we were all having our cup of tea in granny's room, and of course mother could think of nothing but the court. Her mind was filled with memories of the solemn court; you could nearly see its panelled walls rising up around us, dwarfing the small room.

'Michael, you should have seen it. He had a solicitor there, and as if that wasn't enough, a barrister to speak for him, with a wig! Another baldy I expect — oh, a sneering little fellow. He said his client had never refused intercourse but that the plaintiff had, or words to that effect — so I was entitled to nothing! Well I ask you!'

Granny clicked her tongue impatiently.

'Then — wait'll I tell yous — the oul judge put his head down, and sis he out of the long scrawny neck of him, sis he: "Did you refuse to have intercourse with this man — your husband?"'

'Well I gave him his answer, quick enough. "I don't want to have anything to do with him," says I, and the old fellow sits back — the judge, I

130

mean. But wait'll I tell you. I haven't told yous the best part of it yet.'

Mother put her cup down and sat perfectly erect, with a very severe expression. This was the way her solicitor, P. H. O'Reilly, had sat. He was to plead for her, but there was nothing pleading about *him*! mother said.

'He's more of a barrister than a solicitor, I think. Oh, he was a lovely man! Not a stir out of him till at last he stood up. Such contempt in his face! "My client," he says, taking hold of the front of his black dress, "is asking for twenty-five shillings per week. Her husband has given her nothing, not one penny!" Oh, he was dead nuts on winning the case — he spoke up something powerful.'

'And are you getting the money?' I asked.

'Of course,' mother said. 'And what's more I'll have charge of the children. Custardy, they call it.'

Suddenly I had a wonderful feeling of relief. At last the rows were finished with, it seemed. We would all be making a new beginning.

Mother said she would try to find a place out of it. For the present herself and us children lived in the middle room, that used to be the bedroom. *He* lived and slept now in the Far Room and tied his door up with cord when he went out. Well at any rate there would be peace and quiet now, Nana said. The postman had brought my prize, a book, which was a kind of proof that I could write. Yet I was doubtful; the other children's essays were inclined to wander nowhere, just like mine.

Kevin's Corner was a soft target, it seemed. You couldn't miss. So whenever I posted off a painting or a story it was sure to bring a new book in the letter-box. I would be disappointed if I got only the Second Prize.

Granny explained that Kevin could hardly give me First Prize every time. It wouldn't look right, and it wouldn't be fair to the others. 'And now,' she said, 'kneel down at the altar and give thanks to God for what you've got.'

School was fine now; I was hardly ever punished. One time Mr McManus had to slap me for not knowing Irish, but he drew out his strap reluctantly and barely tipped my hand. It made me feel horribly humiliated; it was an affront to my dignity. Was I not a writer, a prize-winner? True, I had uneasy doubts and often marvelled at my luck, yet I became in my own mind a rather unusual boy.

Ronan and I had a quarrel. Each remained haughtily withdrawn, and we were self-consciously 'not speaking'. Just then we were moving to Sixth Standard in a bigger room, and Ronan and I chose to sit in different desks. My new desk-mate was a fair-haired boy who had a pallid skin, and lice used to crawl on his jersey.

Mr McManus seemed to know about the quarrel between Ronan and me. He put us both in the same desk again. I was more than glad, but for fear of betraying too much relief I frowned a little. It was Friday. Well, Monday will soon come round, I thought, and then I can be friends again with Ronan.

On Sunday Maggie asked me would I come with her to Dalkey, and out of politeness I agreed. It was rather a bore going anywhere with Maggie; I felt I had outgrown her every way. Still she had always been for my good. The Dalkey tram ran through Clare Street so we went on a tram, up on top, for a change.

The tram was a racketty, rocky old thing and I felt slightly sick. There was a strong breeze in our faces. Maggie kept holding her hat, looking ahead with half-shut eyes and wryly compressed lips. 'Ah, good old Dalkey!' she said approvingly as the tram lurched to a final stop.

I had often noticed my aunt's annoying habit of repeating old familiar phrases, like this one about Dalkey. There were hundreds of them. For example about draughts. She would say: 'There's a draught from that door that would shave a brass monkey.'

Right enough, as we were getting off the tram Maggie remarked: 'There was a breeze blowing there that would shave a brass monkey!'

What had brass monkeys to do with draughts, I thought sullenly, walking beside her. Only a few days before, as I stood at his desk, Mr O'Neill had reached out and plucked at the dark hairs of my upper lip. 'Did you feel that?' he said, amused. I could feel my face burning with shame and confusion. For months there had been a warm, tickly feeling there, then I had noticed the dark shadow over my lips. It must be obvious to everyone!

I was just as glad that we might not be visiting the two women. Apparently there was a coolness between Maggie and the Little Woman about something she'd said to my granny. Always these bitchy rows were going on. And here in Bessie's there was another coolness between aunt Bessie and uncle Joe, who still insisted that he wanted to get married.

To avoid the grumbling Maggie said we'd sit out in the front garden. 'There's a nice bit of shelter there and we'd be in the sun,' she said, and motioned me to carry out a chair.

Anybody passing might well have thought it was a peaceful picture: the quaint little cottage, the low hedge, two people sitting in the garden talking.

But my aunt was saying something she had planned to say. I still felt enough of the early fear of Maggie to be impressed. When she was in a determined mood there was no gainsaying Maggie.

'Now that you're fourteen,' she told me, 'you'll have to be thinking of work. You'll be fourteen tomorrow.'

I was thunderstruck. 'You mean... You mean I should leave school?'

'Well, you can't stay at school after fourteen. Jobs are scarce, and you'll have to find something to do. You need to start learning a trade at fourteen.'

'But I couldn't leave now, Maggie. I couldn't.'

She sat there, hands folded on her lap, her lips compressed, her blue eyes cold. It was impossible to tell her about Ronan, and how Mr McManus had put us in the same desk again. If I left now it would seem very pointed, as though I resented what Mr McManus had done and was leaving in a huff. Besides I liked school; I wanted to stay on in Sixth, learning something at last. What really irked me, though, was the thought that both Mr McManus and Ronan would feel hurt.

'Maggie, I'd rather not leave school.'

'You must think of the future,' Maggie said. 'Believe me, I know what I'm talking about. Let you go in first thing tomorrow morning and see the headmaster about a reference. If he says anything, just tell him you are fourteen.'

She was just as determined to have me leave as she had been to make me go to school in the first place. She had been right at that time, but now... It was wrong and unfair. I lacked the confidence to tell her that, and in my heart of hearts I felt sure that my aunt knew best. It was the voice of destiny that spoke to me.

On Monday morning I knocked boldly on Mr O'Neill's door. For the moment I had a feeling of freedom and power. He looked up from his desk.

'Sir, I wanted a reference.'

He seemed surprised. 'You want a reference? A character reference? What for?'

'You see, sir, I'm leaving today — now. Because I'm fourteen today.'

'So. You are fourteen,' he said, 'and you want to leave school. Well, well, well!'

'It's not that I want to leave, sir. I have to leave, if I'm to get a trade. The age limit is fourteen.'

He sat gazing before him for a moment, then gave two quick little nods. Then he screwed the cap off his fountain-pen and was busy writing my reference in his tidy, clear hand. Standing beside him I could read a phrase here and there as a gold nib flowed across the pale blue paper:

133

...glad to be able to bear... obedient and straightforward... He is of an artistic temperament but I am sure... disposition calm and steady...

Mr O'Neill bade me good-bye, shaking hands.

I gently closed his door and turned to the long flight of stairs leading down. The mood of elation and freedom had vanished. I felt humiliated and depressed. I began to go down the stairs slowly, thought of looking in to Mr McManus to say good-bye, but lacked the nerve to do it.

It was depressing to think of Mr McManus and my friend Ronan. They would surely, if only for an hour or so, feel snubbed. It was depressing to know that Mr O'Neill had been annoyed at my leaving, the very day I had reached fourteen. It was depressing to feel the finality of going down these familiar stairs for the last time. A surge of resentment nearly choked me. I felt a fierce hatred of Maggie. I had been forced to leave school — compelled to go, although my wishes were far otherwise. It was like Roseville again, I thought bitterly, a place I had loved, yet had been forced to leave.

Self-pity gripped me. I thought of myself in the beautiful house, in that lovely garden. We had been happy there. Yes, we. Granny and Maggie, too, had loved that house and garden.

A feeling of pity for all three of us welled up in me, and I thought of my father and mother too, my brothers and my sister. The city, the whole world was full of strife and misery. A feeling of desolation welled up so overpoweringly that tears came to my eyes.

Through the tears I imagined I saw Sandymount Avenue. So vivid was the memory of that world of sun-struck, level shadows that I'd forgotten I was going down the stairs. Instead, with each step down, came a strange sensation of becoming smaller, very small, as when with Nana long ago I saw the gate. Dark green like holly-leaves it was and higher than my head, but its beshadowed panels were radiant still, like a loving and welcoming smile.

ACKNOWLEDGEMENTS

Some of the details in 'War Comes to Dublin' appeared in the *Irish Times*; 'Aunt Maggie's Romance' was broadcast as a short story on BBC Radio 4.